DYNAMIC TEACHING
in the ELEMENTARY SCHOOL

LEARNING REINFORCEMENT

THE ADMINISTRATIVE REALM

DYNAMIC TEACHING
in the ELEMENTARY SCHOOL

COMPILED BY

Myra B. Cook

Joseph H. Caldwell

Lina J. Christiansen

DRAWINGS BY

Myra B. Cook

PARKER PUBLISHING CO., INC.   WEST NYACK, N.Y.

DEDICATION

To Dean Kimball Wiles who devoted his life to excellence in education.

A WORD FROM THE AUTHORS . . .

Experienced teacher, student teacher, beginning teacher—all of us are striving to bring dynamic teaching to the classroom. Many highly qualified individuals have shared their experiences in this book as they describe their ideas on education. Each chapter has been developed by its author as he perceived his role in teaching children and using methods he found successful. Thus, each discussion might serve as a starting point for your own beginning or renewed efforts in creative teaching.

When you are hard at work with children or pausing to reflect on your influential role as a teacher, we sincerely hope that these experiences, individual philosophies and ideas will help you and your pupils to achieve the excellence in education which is possible in a stimulating teaching situation.

—The Authors

ACKNOWLEDGMENTS

We are grateful to Mr. George Hoffmeier and fifth graders for their work with the activities in *The Senses: Tools for Learning* and to Mr. Alan R. Morris, Director of Public Relations, WJZ-TV, Baltimore for his photographic assistance with *Television and the Classroom Teacher*. Special thanks to Mr. and Mrs. J. R. Brown, Mrs. Blanche Long, Mrs. Shirley McGurran, Mrs. Bernice Green, and to Mrs. Janet Kulesa who typed the manuscript. Also we wish to thank the following for their time and effort in making photographs possible: Cecil Baldus, Tom Ellis, Sheri Fogg, Betty McMillin, Laura Roland, Paul Roland, Julie Stout, Teddy Willi, and Tim Willi.

Acknowledgment is gratefully made to the following copyright holders for permission to reprint from previously published materials:

American-Korean Foundation, Care, Inc., Christian Children's Fund, Compassion, Inc., Foster Parents Plan, Inc., Missionhurst, Project Concern, Inc. and the Save The Children Federation for the use of their photographic material.

Bantam Books for an excerpt from *The Medium Is the Message* by Marshall McLuhan and Quention Fiore. Copyright 1967.

The *Florida Times-Union—Jacksonville Journal* for reprinting an article on installation of the Florida-Virgin Island telephone cable, Mr. John Leach for the use of his news article and Mr. Ray Stafford for the photographs accompanying this article.

Kalakshetra Publications for an excerpt from *The Discovery of the Child* by Maria Montessori. Copyright 1966.

The Macmillan Company for an excerpt from *A Perfect Education* by Kenneth E. Eble. Copyright 1966.

G. Schirmer, Inc. for the words and music to "Marching to Pretoria" in *Songs from the Veld* by Josef Marais. Copyright 1942.

Schocken Books, Inc. for an excerpt from *The Montessori Method* by Maria Montessori. Copyright 1964.

Simon and Schuster, Inc. for an excerpt from *Teacher* by Sylvia Ashton-Warner. Copyright 1963.

The Authors

CONTENTS

MATHEMATICS

SCIENCE

SOCIAL STUDIES

AUDIO-VISUAL OPPORTUNITIES

DYNAMIC TEACHING
in the ELEMENTARY SCHOOL

1

Characteristics of Creativity
in Childhood Education

Dr. Helen L. Merrill

ABOUT THE AUTHOR

Helen L. Merrill holds the Bachelor of Arts degree from Asbury College, the Master of Arts from Florida State University and the Doctor of Education from the University of Maryland. During her 36 years in education, she has served in numerous positions including elementary-secondary principal, secondary science and English teacher, and university professor and dean. In addition, Dr. Merrill has taught television courses and served as a special representative of President Lyndon Johnson to the Guatemalan Trade Fair. Her publications include the book *Science Teacher in Action*, and the articles, *"Motivation"* and *"A Physical Science Course for General Education."* She is presently County Coordinator of Secondary Education.

Good teaching is not to be confused with creativity in teaching. Though one may lead to the other, the end product is different.

Good teaching, in recognition of the varying abilities of the children, means teaching at several levels. There is that teaching which consists principally of facts, often learned by rote, with a subsequent regurgitation of these facts. Some children cannot respond beyond this stage, but too many who could are left there by uninspired teachers. A teacher of my acquaintance was asked in mid-October by fifth grader Glenn Smith, "Miss Holmes, am I going to pass?" "Why, Glenn, I don't know. It depends on how you do." "I'm doing just like I'm gonna be doing," replied the uninspired boy.

17

Teaching for understanding is the next step up and it is at this level that a superior teacher functions. The step above this is the creative stage.

Creativity in teaching the young is possible for all teachers—though some will be more effective than others. Creativity cannot be taught directly but, as with the most satisfying and elevated areas of life, must be taught by indirection. The teacher provides the opportunity to the young for experiences, both inward and outward, that foster the motivational climate of creativity. This process is highly individual both as to preparation and procedures. A seven-year-old of my acquaintance has a wise and wonderful grandmother who is a school administrator. While the grandmother and I were working on a project the child sometimes interrupted to ask questions. The grandmother suggested three things that she could do in an adjoining room and added "What shall you do?" The little girl replied "I guess I'll write a poem called "What Shall I Do?"

In about twenty minutes she returned with her poem which (after a minor revision by her) reads as follows.

What shall I do?
Shall I hoot like an owl?
Shall I run like a squirrel?
Shall I fly like a bat?
Shall I purr like a cat?
I sat and I thought one sunny day.
Shall I run like a bay?
Why don't I kick and kick?

This creative effort was possible because of the interaction of many factors or experiences, some minor, some major. She has parents who arrange for all four of their children to have varied experiences, including visits to museums and historical sites. The child had been encouraged to read good but simple poetry and prose. These also had been read to her. Then, too, she is in a school that does not discourage individual efforts.

In addition, the seven-year-old had had the advantage of frequent association with the grandmother who is not harried by the care of other youngsters. Finally, playtime with her peers is not pre-empted by sometimes foolish requests. This potentially creative child has had time to grow, interact with peers and to *live without pressure*.

To the persons responsible for the climate of creativity the rewards are twofold, an exhilaration of the spirit and a personal sense of gratification. When one takes part in a creative effort, the inner man is renewed as in no other way. Further, the personal satisfaction of perceiving this almost awe-inspiring achievement of the young is a recompense without equal.

The teacher who attains creativity in his teaching cannot and should not expect to maintain this top elevation at all times. Creativity can only be based on the discipline of hard work, and here the teacher must make decisions of the effort versus the cost.

The ways and means of producing a creative climate are best understood if creativity is defined and identified as it pertains to the teaching process. First, the child is exposed to a range of experiences which may be manual and body skills, intellectual, esthetic, spiritual and social learning, or contacts with formerly unknown areas of everyday living. Out of the digestive and absorption processes comes a new product, either material or nonmaterial, that can be made known to others. This product may be entirely new or simply a new combination. To illustrate, children may have learned to manipulate modeling clay; during this time language skills and mathematical skills have been developed; perhaps a play given by another grade level has been enjoyed. In the reading period the emphasis may have been on Early America. Now a most important element is interspersed—time to do as one pleases *without even the most subtle of pressures*. Perhaps nothing will come of this time but perhaps a child who has never seen a beaver will imagine and mold one in clay; another might write a playlet about an Indian child who stole a beaver from captivity to set it free. Familiar material will constitute essential parts of the whole but the result will be something qualitatively new. "For the learner (if not for the world) actual creation has taken place."[1]

It is not true, however, that children are merely turned loose to pursue their own interests, until some conclusions are reached regarding the importance of working as individuals and the unworthiness of parroting others. This applies to the kindergarten and primary grades as well as to older children. There must be guiding activities so that standards for using materials are established and the protection of the rights of others are recognized. These ground rules are effective only when the children are involved in setting up the code of behavior. A self-educated man I knew many years ago advised me in country parlance about relationship with the young. He said "Never buy a dog and then do your own barking." The discipline of short but firm commitments *carried out* is often the framework of individual and perhaps creative work by a young person. Hopefully, one of the natural outcomes of the creative act would be an atmosphere of mutual respect and understanding—an emotional climate where unique human beings are valued.

Creativity may receive a setback when young people arrive at the stage where they feel that conformity to peer group standards is all-important.

[1]William H. Kilpatrick, "The Place of Creating in the Educational Process," Childhood Education, 7:116 (Nov., 1930).

A teacher can only wait for the crisis to pass and during this period continue to value the original or the creative. In this atmosphere the young person will ultimately learn to think for himself and make his own judgments.

The compensation to the master teacher for all of the thoughtful interest and work involved in maintaining a creative climate is both inward and outward. For his own gratification he has the knowledge of self-development. He has also that most rewarding and exhilarating experience—that of having stimulated a child's ability to create.

2

$\mathcal{D}$iscovering $\mathcal{I}$ndividual $\mathcal{L}$earning $\mathcal{S}$tyles

Judith M. Eddinger

ABOUT THE AUTHOR

Judy Eddinger received her Bachelor of Science degree from the University of Alabama and has attended the University of Florida, Stetson University, Jacksonville University, Southern Methodist University and the University of Alaska. In 1966 she was a recipient of the Valley Forge Teaching Medal. After working in the field of advertising and public relations for several years, she began her teaching career and has experience totaling 12 years at the elementary level. She has published articles in *The Instructor, Grade Teacher,* the *Florida Education Journal,* the *Alaskan Teacher* and a series of by-line articles on teaching in the *Anchorage Daily News.*

You may be a dynamic teacher with an exciting program that stimulates the majority of your students. And yet, some of your pupils lack the skills or the interest to stay in the mainstream of learning. And you wonder—how do I reach *them?*

There is Mark whose IQ is high and whose performance is low. Do you write on his report card—*Mark does not work up to his ability*—and expect his parents either to do something about Mark's laziness or to accept it?

There is Susan, who seems to have average ability, but who is so shy she won't enter into discussions and always evades standing up and speaking before the class. Do you write on her report card—*Susan should participate more in class*—and expect her parents to speak to Susan about being a more sparkling, outgoing individual during the next six week grading period?

21

What about Eric? Is he the one about whom you say—*Immature—recommend that he be retained at this grade level*?

Then there is Jeff who daydreams, and also, Jennifer who is easily distracted. Do you just label them as dreamers and expect the next teacher to devise a way of bringing them to the threshold of reality? After all, most of your students are progressing beautifully. Should you worry about a few who are not?

These children who seem to be "lost in the shuffle" of regular classrooms need the attention and guidance of a person who is primarily interested in protecting them from just such categories as *immature, lazy, disorganized, daydreamer, nonconformist, shy and withdrawn.*

In a traditionally graded school structure one possibility may be in forming small classes on grade levels for the purpose of helping these individuals discover their own learning styles. It would be a challenge to many teachers, and you, with your proven success of reaching so many children, might be just the teacher to work with such a class.

If separate classes *cannot* be formed, you can still reach these children by organizing your classroom along certain lines.

Seating Arrangements

If you can set up a separate class, ideally it should not include more than twenty pupils. The seating arrangement should be flexible. Circles of four or five desks make it easier for the teacher to draw up a chair and help several children at the same time.

- Such groupings are convenient for math instruction and group reading.
- Committee meetings and projects can be carried on easily without disrupting the entire seating arrangements.
- If a child needs to work alone or if an activity calls for pairing off, the desks can simply be pulled aside.

Individual Needs

After arranging the room to best meet the needs of the group, your next step is to find out what each *individual* need might be. Diagnostic tests will help tell you what the child does and does not know, but keen observation will help you discover *how* he learns. Take time to study the reaction to some of your activities, but remember: do not be misled by a lively response from some of your pupils. Encouraged by their enthusiasm, it is easy to think the whole class is breezing along with you. As always, there are a few who are confused or distracted. They must be reached another day or another way. Another way is preferable since going over the same material in the same way tends to dull the interest of the minds you once held captive.

Individual Learning Styles

As you experiment with teaching techniques, don't chuck all of your old tried and true methods. They may work like a charm for some children. For instance, a certain child may master his spelling words by writing them five times each, while many children go through the motions and have not retained a thing. The old-fashioned spelling bee is often an exciting challenge to good spellers. To the poor speller it is an agonizing experience, unless he can come up with an innovation such as one little fellow who suggested to his teacher, "Instead of making us sit down when we miss a word, why don't you let *us* go to the end of the line, too—so we can try again on a new word?"

In another class the children appeared to be enjoying a record which taught the multiplication facts by musical verse. In frustration one boy blurted out, "I just hate that man on the record when he laughs and says, 'If you didn't get them all right this time, let's try it again!' " Obviously, this child was not enjoying or benefiting from the musical drill as much as his classmates.

- Some children absorb information through reading. It takes a film to give meaning to the same material for others.
- Some children learn from listening while others have not developed good listening habits.
- Some children need long blocks of time to get assignments completed. Others work quickly.
- Some children may work compatibly in pairs—some in larger groups. Still others work best alone.

Vary your techniques and observe your class in action. Let your children know that you are trying to find the best way for them to learn. They may come up with some ideas themselves.

Parental Support

Never underestimate the ability of parents to assist you in this undertaking. Meet with them in a group to fully explain your goals and objectives.

- Be sure they have a positive and optimistic attitude about the class. They should not be given the impression that this is a group of slow learners or that these children are going to be allowed to simply play around while others in the same grade are taught discipline and good study habits in their classrooms.

- You must convince these parents that you want their children to work just as hard and have just as much success as any other group of children. Once they realize that you are sincere in your beliefs that possibly some of the pressure of working for grades and competing with others must be lifted before these children can begin to succeed, you have won a major battle. Attitudes are catching, as everyone knows.

If the parents appreciate your eagerness to help their children enjoy school and learn for the sake of learning, they will be happy. Happy parents, happy children, happy teacher!

Home Visits

Since it is a small class and you want the full support of the parents, it would be wise to visit in their homes. Don't make it a visit to try to discover exactly why the child is like he is. (Although you may get some very good insights into the child's background.) Make it a friendly visit just to get better acquainted with the child and his parents. One way is to explain to the parents your plan to make a couple of visits each week.

- Call mother in advance and ask if you might bring the child home after school and visit with her.
- Thirty minutes over a cup of coffee can do wonders to strengthen the relationship between parent and teacher.
- The father may want to be at home when you visit and if he can't arrange to be there in the afternoon, possibly they will invite you to come in the evening.

Classroom Visits

Next, set aside one hour a week for the parents to visit your classroom. Make it a standing invitation for them to feel free to come at this time. It will not be necessary to have anything special or showy planned for them; however, if you have a particularly interesting lesson or activity where all children are involved, it would be nice to schedule it at this time.

- Let these parents take some of the responsibility of finding out just how their children work and learn.

Evaluation—Grades

Don't grade papers. Since you are going to give all these children all the individual help you possibly can, and you are expecting them to do some of their work in pairs or in small groups, the advantage of grading paper work is doubtful.

- Why not mark their mistakes and let the children correct them? Encourage perfect papers, of course. You might give 100% on all perfect papers and *100% corrected* on their other papers.
- If each child has a manila folder he can be responsible for filing his own perfect papers and the papers he has corrected.
- A discarded wire phonograph record rack, placed on a work table, is ideal for holding folders. With the folders arranged alphabetically it is easily accessible to the children, the teacher, and the parents when they come to visit.
- When the parent has an opportunity to look over the papers and see that an effort is being made to learn from mistakes and to improve the quality of handwriting, spelling and grammar, he will be inclined more than ever to support you. So often only the good papers are brought home by the children anyway, and many times when poor papers are delivered it is impossible for the parents to analyze the errors and make this a learning situation for the child.
- Don't send report cards either—if you can justify your reasons to school administrators. You have established good rapport with the children's parents. They have a standing invitation to visit your classroom once a week. At this time they can examine their child's work and by taking a look around the room have a fairly good idea of the activities in progress. They are aware of their child's particular problem and have confidence in your desire to solve it. They know that a private conference with the teacher, which should be scheduled periodically, will reveal any new problems.
- A narrative explanation of the child's progress might be sent home, but the standard report card, which is created to show the child's standing in each subject as compared with others in his class, is simply defeating your purpose.

The Reading Program

In working with these children an individualized reading program is a must. If you have always taught reading in the three traditional groups of high, medium and low, and you don't know how you are going to manage your time or keep track of progress on each child, get some of the latest books on this subject and after a careful study and plan of action make the plunge. You'll find that once you are meeting the child's individual reading needs, other areas of growth will follow more naturally.

- Read aloud as many books as you possibly can to your children.
- Occasionally, you could read an exciting part of a book to whet the child's appetite for finishing it.

- Take a child aside and read to him while the others are working. If it is a younger child, you might read a short book in its entirety. If it is an older child you might want to share a paragraph or two from a longer book you think he might enjoy.
- Make a book tree of all the books that *WE* have read—the ones you read aloud and the ones they have read. You can find a perfect branch from a tree to make your own indoor book tree. Pot it and paint it a gay color. When a book has been completed, use a plain white file card to print on the name and author. Attach some sort of symbol to identify the book. It may be a trinket such as found in a Crackerjack box or something you have made from construction paper, clay or cloth. The card bearing *Charlotte's Web* by E. B. White would be greatly enhanced by one of the rubbery spiders sold in novelty stores. *Strawberry Girl* by Lois Lensky might have a tiny strawberry made of plastic or clay. You will enjoy watching the book tree grow and it will make an attractive display in the school library toward the end of the year.

Of course there are many other ways to encourage children to keep a record of the books they have read. You will discover those when you read all those good books on Individualized Reading Instruction!

Spelling

Since the children are reading in different books and obviously have different interests, why not let them select their own spelling words?

- Tape a lined file card on the top of each child's desk. As he encounters a new word or asks for the spelling of a word he needs, let him put the word on his card.
- At the beginning of the week you might test the class on a list of words and be sure that each child places his missed words on his card. Any word that is circled wrong on daily papers should also be jotted down.
- Other sources for words would be spelling texts, dictionaries, encyclopedias or books they are reading.
- When a child has fifteen words on his card, give assignments such as marking the vowel sounds, dividing into syllables, arranging alphabetically, writing sentences or a story.

If each child has an individual list you might wonder how you are going to manage testing each one. (Not that testing the child on his words insures his spelling them correctly forevermore, but it is an indication of how well he has studied them and knows them for the time being at least.)

- Just draw up a chair at one of your circle of desks. Gather up their cards and begin calling out words around the circle . . .

Pam—*cattle*; Chuck—*desert*; Phil—*chalk*; Cindy—*typewriter*, and so on around the circle again. It really goes quickly and when you are finished, collect the papers and put the incorrect words on a fresh card to be taped to the desk again.
- File the old cards in a central file box under the child's name. Give a review test every two weeks on thirty words.

The children derive much satisfaction out of choosing their own words and you will soon notice that they are attempting to master more difficult words all the time. Some children will be able to compile two lists for testing each week. Each child should have at least one list called out to him each week. •

Creative Writing

Give some kind of creative writing assignment every day and observe how each child tackles the problem.

- Does he say, "I can't think"? Then help him get started by asking him questions and giving him a few suggestions.
- Does he say, "I don't know how to write down what I'm thinking"? Then help him by letting him dictate his thoughts to you while you write them. (A typewriter is handy for this type of help.)
- On one day work with a circle of children who need help with spelling, punctuation and grammar. The next day work with a group which needs ideas and inspiration. Work in small groups discussing descriptive words and phrases.
- Give children plenty of time to finish any type of writing, but don't let them fool around and make excuses for not finishing. You might say, "We are going to write for twenty minutes and I want you to concentrate very hard on your topic. At the end of twenty minutes I will ask you to put your work up so that we can go on to something else. Later you will have time to finish." Some children will get good results this way. Others will do better if you let them alone to finish their writing at one sitting. Be careful to notice these tendencies, and in time you will understand how each child produces his best work. You may expect to receive a good paper from Joe in half an hour, and you may know that Jim has just begun to get his thoughts organized by this time and that his work will not be ready to be turned in until the next day.
- Let the class work in small groups to write stories or plays.
  - Pair them off to write telephone conversations or dialogue between two people in an interesting situation.
  - Let them put their stories or plays on tape or compile their works into a class book.

- Discuss a new word that you want them to add to
  their vocabulary each day and have them include
  that in their writing. At the end of the week review
  the words and ask them to tie them together in a
  meaningful story.
- Tell them to write a paragraph with no punctuation. Let them
  exchange papers to punctuate correctly.
- Build a file of pictures that inspire good stories and build a list of
  interesting topics that are easy to write about. *The Nicest Room
  in My House—I Dreamed Lincoln Came to Visit Our Classroom
  —If I Had a Million Dollars—The Nicest Person on My Street
  —How We Entertain Out-of-Town Visitors.* You'll think of more
  topics and they'll think of some too. But every day be sure that
  they have the chance to express themselves in writing.
- Let them keep their work in folders. One day's assignment might
  be to rewrite one of their paragraphs or stories. Make writing as
  pleasurable a habit as reading.

Social Studies

To make children more aware of their world today—to build interest in
people, places and events—make use of the daily newspapers. This most-
current-of-all textbooks can approach Social Studies from the here and now
—giving children motivation for studying the past and a foundation for
understanding the future.

That most-current-of-all textbooks, the newspaper, gives children
motivation for studying the past and a foundation for understanding the future.

- In some cities the newspaper offers a program of study and will deliver a paper for each child in the class at a very low cost. If this is not possible some of the children may be able to bring in the family newspaper. Although you have only your own daily newspaper to work with, you can create an interest in current events and teach the children how to read a newspaper.
- Be sure they are familiar with the different sections of the paper.
  - Can they distinguish between a news story and an editorial? Let them have practice in looking up facts and forming opinions.
  - Teach them how to write a news story using the *who? what? when? where? why? how?*
  - Involve them in some role playing by letting them act out an event such as a fire:
    - *The news reporter accompanied by photographer arrives on the scene of the fire.*
    - *He gets his facts from observation and from the firemen and witnesses who vividly describe the action.*
    - *He calls the information into the city desk where it is taken down and written up for the press.*
  - An actual trip to the newspaper publishing company will help clarify the many processes that are involved from the time an event occurs until it appears in the paper.
- Have the class keep abreast of the headlines and major happenings that occur locally, nationally and internationally.
  - Clip pictures of city, state and world leaders. Have children bring in different shots of the famous faces that appear in *Time, Newsweek, Look* and other magazines. Mount the pictures on heavy paper and use them for flash card quizzes to test the children on their familiarity with these prominent figures.
- Always discuss the news with the appropriate map or globe available so that the cities, states or countries can be located.
  - Keep a vocabulary listing on a special part of the board under the heading *People, Places and Words in the News This Week.*
  - Make a scrapbook of the most outstanding front page stories of the week.
- Bring in papers from other cities and compare the style and format.
- Follow up the news on radio and television.
- Study the want-ads and write make-believe letters applying for jobs listed in the help-wanted section.
- Study the ads. Make up a grocery list and check the prices in the weekend specials.

There are endless possibilities for enriching every subject through this inexpensive and very timely medium. Remember, of course, that what holds fascination and interest for some of your students may not bring forth the same response from others. By centering your attention on just a few pupils at a time you will better be able to provide the lead-up activities and skill building exercises necessary for holding their attention. For instance, one day you might discuss a front page event with four or five children and then let them report it to the rest of the group. By talking things over in small groups you can be sure of reaching all.

Science

With Science, as with Social Studies, this group of children, who for one reason or another, has not achieved expected goals, is not going to dutifully read the text, watch the teacher perform a couple of experiments and then take the chapter test and pass it with flying colors.

- These children must be given many opportunities to learn for themselves—to become involved in processes of observing, communicating, measuring, inferring, and predicting.
- Your circle of desks will be convenient for children to work on projects and discuss basic concepts.
  - For example, in observing growth in plants each child will have his own seeds to plant. He will do his own observing, measuring, and will keep his own record. If he needs help from a classmate or the teacher, he feels free to ask for it and discuss his problem. The point is that he is not told exactly what to do, what is supposed to happen and why. In many different ways, he is given first hand experience to find out for himself.
- You may draw upon your strong relationship with the parents to create interest in individual projects and experiments. Much scientific observation and experimentation can be carried out at home when time, space, and materials are limited at school.
- A child can see in the kitchen examples of friction, steam, gravity, fluids in operation, electricity, chemical reaction and a multitude of other scientific phenomena.
- Often the whole family grows better informed through working together on such projects as gardening, learning to cook or assemble and operate radios. When these experiments are shared in the classroom new interests and hobbies develop naturally for some children. Such a special interest might open up avenues for learning in other subjects. A child who is encouraged to pursue his hobby of having an aquarium might carry over his interest into the areas of reading and writing. This special interest might be the key to his style of learning.

Individual Talents

You'll want to provide a variety of ways for these children to express themselves and to discover individual talents.

- Teach games, songs and rhythmic dances.
- Let them work on choral readings and plays. You may find a lovely voice to compliment or a dramatic flair to cultivate among these children who are used to sitting back and letting someone else be in the limelight.
- You will see leaders emerge through necessity. Someone has to take the main part. Someone has to be the captain. Someone has to be the chairman. You can help them take these roles with pride and confidence as you work with them individually and in small groups.

Keep in mind that you are constantly trying to help each child find his own path to success. It may very well be through art or dramatics. It may be through sports or academic achievement. The important thing is that mutual respect and improved attitudes have a chance to flourish in the classroom so that desired learning goals for all can be reached.

In such an atmosphere it should soon dawn on the child that much of the responsibility for his success in learning is his to assume. This will not be such an overwhelming burden but will become a pleasurable challenge because you have let him find the way that is best for him. You have taught him to compete with his own record so that competition of others is no longer a threat to his progress. You have protected him from useless criticism. You have helped him to see his strengths and to build on them.

As the year progresses you will find that you are probably giving less individual instruction—that common bonds have been reached, and that your class is working more as a unit. This could mean that most of these children have gained the independence and the motivation to work in almost any good classroom situation.

3

Off to a Good Start

Sister Mary Gilbert, S.S.N.D.

ABOUT THE AUTHOR

Sister Mary Gilbert received the degree of Bachelor of Science in Education from the College of Notre Dame of Maryland in Baltimore. She has completed graduate work with Hunter College, Catholic University and Columbia University. Sister has taught in the elementary school for 35 years and is presently a first grade teacher at the Notre Dame Preparatory School in Towson, Maryland. Her article *"Not Only at Christmas"* was published in *Catholic School Journal.*

For the primary teacher preparing to meet the little ones who will be in her care during the school year, who has met class after class of children now growing up and continuing their education (or even, perhaps, as parents sending their youngsters to begin their formal schooling in her room), the days preceding school are busy and happy ones. Such a teacher knows the importance of being ready to welcome the children into a room which they will quickly recognize as theirs, a room which they will look forward to entering each morning of the school year because they will soon know that here their natural propensity for learning will be satisfied.

The Atmosphere

- Fresh flowers and an abundance of attractive picture books, learning games and math apparatus, including the perenially useful flannel board, lure the early arrivals.

- Desks are labelled with names lettered on brightly colored cards, with a flower, bird, or some other gay seal beside it, helping those who cannot yet recognize the name to easily locate a locker similarly marked.
- Folders with pockets for carrying papers, primary magazines, messages, etc. have been labelled, to be distributed as a first lesson in courteously accepting and thanking—as well as a means for again comparing names. (Many children know how to letter names only with capitals, so to present lower case letters is the "grown-up" way of name recognition and writing, and how they do love to be grown-up!)
- Bulletin boards, I have always thought, should be very simple for young children: a few attractive colored pictures, several short sentences or words for each picture, perhaps some alphabet cards, all large and clear enough to be seen easily from all points in the room.

> *I preview pictures to be posted by placing them on the chalk ledge in front and then sitting in the last row to make my choice. Of course, smaller pictures may be used on bulletin boards which are not directly in front, provided the children have easy access to them or can be seated close by when they are discussed.*

The School Day

Each child has a box of one-inch colored cubes in his desk and another empty box (labelled) to receive the Dolch picture and word cards. All of these cards have been sorted, rubber-banded in packs of thirty, and arranged alphabetically in shoe boxes for use in reading lessons. Each individual word card is given to the child as that word is taught. Preparation before the first day does take hours, but I've found the results highly gratifying. How easy it is later to take out a pack of "mother" cards and distribute one to each child! And how enthusiastic the children are about their growing reading vocabulary of which they have so concrete a form!

- Homework for the first months is "Study your word cards," and eager beavers often surprise one by saying, "I can spell every word in my box." And they can! An incentive to others, too!

As school progresses, the largest part of the school day is devoted to the language arts, with reading as the center. Comprehension is, of course, the goal of reading, as it is a primary key to future study.

- The use of the library is begun immediately so that the child will love and appreciate good reading from the start.

- An analytic-synthetic method of phonics is studied as one of the many means to building a reading vocabulary. This method begins with auditory discrimination and is followed by visual analysis of word forms. Following the principle of going from the known to the unknown, beginning reading is based on the child's *speaking vocabulary*, which is logically enlarged by giving many opportunities for oral expression, for listening to stories, poems, and answers to some of the many "Why's" the child's natural curiosity prompts.

- We do, in fact, try to *encourage* the "Why's" by an experimental approach to science, thus helping children to discover for themselves the answers to many of their questions, as well as to formulate others. As an example, plant growth and reproduction, from seed to seed, is an experiment enthusiastically participated in by little ones:

    > *Each child plants some flower or vegetable*
    > *seeds in his own small pot (I save the plastic*
    > *cups for hot drinks and punch a hole in the*
    > *bottom of each). He cares for the plants over*
    > *a period of several months, and then takes them*
    > *home to window-sill or garden. A lima bean*
    > *plant produced blossoms and beans which were*
    > *actually cooked in the school kitchen and eaten*
    > *for luncheon. Remark: "I never liked beans be-*
    > *fore, but I do now!"*

- *Such a science experiment was a means of integrating:*
  Reading—from text and supplementary science books;
  Oral Language—spontaneously used as observation of growth of
    the different plants continued day by day;
  The growth of a sense of responsibility in the care of the plants;
  Short written records based on observation.

Correct stroke sequence in manuscript writing is taught by having the children trace, in the air (on their magic blackboards) the large letters being made on the blackboard by the teacher. This kinesthetic appeal, repeated over and over in both writing and word and letter recognition, is very valuable in assisting even the slowest learner; because the child is following the teacher's stroke sequence *as* she is forming the letters, not copying previously prepared material which any primary teacher knows may be done backwards or even upside-down; thus, incorrect learning is prevented at the source.

Often we have heard, "An ounce of prevention is worth a pound of cure," thus a good teacher must foresee difficulties, eliminate needless ones, present others *one at a time*, so the small child can feel success, and as we continue to strive to make success possible for all our pupils, each reaching for the fulfillment of his own potential, the "beginnings" should flower into "ends" truly worthy of the humanity so richly endowed by God.

TEACHER'S NOTEBOOK

1. If children do not have enough successful experiences, they lose their inner drive to learn. Feeling good about one's self is denied to many children.
2. Nothing gives children a better feeling about themselves than being able to do something correctly—and finish it correctly without help from others. Give children a way to verify things for themselves.
3. Mistakes are important. No one learns without mistakes.
4. Mistakes disappear quickly with a magic slate or a chalkboard slate. Practice. Practice.
5. Anything we cannot cope with, we begin to dislike. It is the same with children.
6. The most important thing in learning is to complete a job.
7. A child cannot be creative unless he has fundamentals to work with. Haphazard experimentation is not creativity.
8. The geography of the classroom is important if children will learn to be orderly.
9. Youngsters need a place of their own—their desk, their locker, their shelf, their drawer.
10. Treat children's own words and expressions with great respect.
11. Encourage children to make their own books, their own stories.
12. Isolate exactly what you want to teach. Do not clutter your lessons. Define the work. Use a minimum of words in presenting the material. Most adults give too many directions to children. Eliminate distractions.
13. Instill respect in children—respect for work, for individuals, for service to others, for each person's role in the society.
14. In order to survive as a society, we must learn to obey. Children must learn to obey.
15. Generally speaking, the progression in workbooks is too fast, too complicated. Watch for this. Simplify the presentation.
16. One workbook can do for several children if you cover the page with an acetate sheet and work with grease pencil.
17. Games do not have the same emotional charge as a lesson. Drive home your lessons through games.

4

Parent-Teacher Rapport: Is It Necessary?

Lina J. Christiansen

ABOUT THE AUTHOR

Lina Christiansen received her Bachelor of Arts degree from Atlantic Union College in Lancaster, Massachusetts. Her twelve years in the classroom include positions in Connecticut, Washington State, New York State and California. She has taught high school, elementary school, multiple and single grades, and Elementary Art, grades 1 through 6. Mrs. Christiansen has given seminars for graduate students at Cornell University and has conducted workshops and television seminars for classroom teachers. She is co-author of the book *The Come-Alive Classroom*.

"I don't like school." "I've got a mean teacher. He isn't fair." "Math is too hard and even when I try, I don't get it." "The boy in back keeps teasing me, but I don't want to say anything because he's the teacher's pet."

How many times have parents heard these, or similar complaints, from their school age children? Should they be ignored? Should the children be upheld—creating tensions—even a "battlefield," with the school and teachers as the enemy? Since school is mandatory for at least ten of the formative years of a child's life, it helps to create the pattern for adult life. Is it one of happiness and accomplishment? Or is it a series of discouragements, unfinished tasks and little personal success—which can lead to withdrawal or aggressiveness?

Good parent-teacher rapport is extremely important for the welfare of the child, the parent and *the teacher*. Here are some suggestions for building a solid relationship between the school and the home.

1. At the beginning of the school year, during the first or second week, send home a brief, mimeographed sheet to the parents.

- Ask if you could enlist their aid for field trips.
- Ask if they have a special interest or hobby the children would enjoy sharing—or do they know someone in the community who does? Make some suggestions. Include a wide range such as,
  - *Story telling, puppetry, marionettes.*
  - *Art interests could include working with clay, decorating pottery, sketching, watercolors, flower arranging, cake decorating. Such demonstrations would be stimulating, and even more fun for the children if they could participate in some small way.*
  - *Music—do they play an instrument; would they give a concert for the class.*
  - *Science—simple experiments demonstrated in class.*
  - *Photography could include simple techniques for getting good composition, showing samples of poorly arranged and well-arranged subjects.*
  - *Ask if any parents have traveled abroad, and if so, to what countries? Do they have slides, movies, realia they would be willing to show?*
- If parents dislike appearing before a group, perhaps they would loan articles that are related to or would enrich their children's studies. (They could specify "May Be Handled" or "Just Look, Please"—children are usually responsive to such signs. Emphasize, however, that things of irreplaceable nature or of sentimental value should not be sent—accidents do happen!)

After making this initial contact with the parents, it is much easier to write another note or to telephone if a minor problem should arise.

2. If you should receive a dinner invitation to a home, you will find the evening a rewarding experience for you, your student and the parents. To see a child in his home environment is very helpful. The teacher becomes a warm person and a closer friend. When a child opens lines of communication between his parents and the teacher, he goes to school in a happy frame of mind, a mind uncluttered by fault-finding and prejudice. This climate is conducive to learning.

3. Encourage parents to discuss the school day with their child, to ask him specific questions, such as: "How did math go today? Did you understand what you were doing? Did you have to be spoken to for talking out of turn? What was your story about in reading today?" Parents should ask questions that the child can answer with some self-esteem.

4. If parents are really unhappy with their child's progress, the atmos-

phere, or specific activities in school, the child will know it. Encourage parents to come to you. Be honest and polite. Confine your discussions to the child. Emphasize the fact that you are working with the parents *and* the child.

5. Give the parent the distinct feeling and confidence that you like each child. State it and feel it. Don't begin teaching with a bias toward a child. Don't let the things you've heard about a child's past record influence you in forming a negative attitude toward him. If the child is a disciplinary problem, talk with him personally and often (not in front of the others). Tell him that you like him and that you have confidence in his ability to be a very worthwhile person.

6. If a child has been a problem in school for several years and upon request the parent comes to you with the attitude of "here we go again. I've heard it year in and year out," suggest that this year will be a fresh sheet and work to strengthen weaknesses and make progress in the right direction. Perhaps not giant strides—but noticeable progress by the year's end.

7. At the beginning of the year, when parents are given the first opportunity to visit the classroom, (Parents Night, Open House, etc.) suggest local places that children would benefit by visiting during the year. Mention that this would enrich their experiences as the classroom units are studied. This could perhaps be suggested as "homework."

8. If a child has accomplished well in a given task, phone the parent and report the good news.

9. Keep a box of notepaper handy. Send a brief note to the parents when a child deserves a word of praise.

10. At Thanksgiving time you might make a simple card with a Thanksgiving motif and write, "I'm thankful for interested and helpful parents." Parents appreciate being remembered if they have been helpful.

11. When having a parent conference and a troubled parent is pouring out personal information that is not relevant to the child's success in school, tactfully stop him. This may be information that he will be sorry at a later time that he divulged. You might say something like, "I sympathize with you but I think we need to concentrate on your child's success in school."

12. If a new child is brought to your room to join the class, although you may already have an oversized class, greet the child warmly, as though he were the first student to arrive. It wasn't his idea to join your class and he needs the reassurance that he is wanted. Tell him you're happy to have him, assign a buddy for a day or two to "show him the ropes." At the beginning of the year tell the children about the "buddy system" for latecoming new class members and stress that it is a privilege and a responsibility to help orient new members as happily as possible.

13. When a parent is in the hospital or has had a long illness, have a

child write a letter or make a card from the class. If a parent has had an honor conferred upon him, a card or letter from a class representative would be appreciated—or use these opportunities as Language Arts activities and ask the whole class to participate. If there was a write-up in the local paper, post the clipping on the bulletin board.

14. When having a parent conference have tea or coffee to offer the parent. Sit in a chair of equal size at a table or desk grouping where papers can be spread out and discussed. Don't sit behind your desk and offer the parent a small chair. This doesn't foster discussion and makes a parent uncomfortable.

15. Get a copy of Haim Ginott's *Between Parent and Child* (MacMillan Publishing Co., 1965). Read it from cover to cover!

Working with students and parents is to a large degree a matter of common sense. The items mentioned above are but a few which may foster a closer personal relationship between the teacher and the parent. The teacher needs to provide an environment of security, and to deal as fairly as possible with all students by considering their personal problems. When insecurity, unhappiness and negative feelings are encountered, positive and happy aspects should be emphasized.

Accomplishing these tasks is not always easy. However, any progress cannot help but pay rich dividends in the future. The key to positive parent-teacher-student relationship, then, may be found in regard for the individual, common sense and the fact that we really depend on, and need, each other's support.

5

The Visually Impaired Child
in a Regular Class

Ann Carroll Weaver

ABOUT THE AUTHOR

Ann Weaver holds the Bachelor of Arts degree from Longwood College in Farmville, Virginia. She is completing work on the Master of Education in Special Education at the University of Virginia. She has had special courses in Braille and in the Education of the Visually Handicapped at Syracuse University. Her teaching experience includes positions as kindergarten and elementary teacher in the Virginia School for the Blind. She is a member of the Council of Exceptional Children and the Association for the Education of the Visually Handicapped.

As more money is appropriated to school systems for the education of exceptional children, and as more teachers are being trained in special education, children with handicaps are being educated in public schools, often, right along with non-handicapped youngsters. These special children, without exception, are entitled to receive an education of and for excellence. They are capable of achieving the goal if given the opportunity.

My special concern is the child who is visually impaired. He may be totally blind, or he may have some limited vision. He may have other handicaps but for the majority of these youngsters in the public school program, blindness is the only impairment. The child can hear well; he has an IQ comparable to those of his peers; he can walk. In short, he can be an independent person if allowed to be, a child like any other child.

The teacher who finds such a child in her class may be upset about how he can possibly give the student special attention he will need. The teacher may let him be a passive member of the class, in which case if he does learn anything, he'll have to do it himself. Or, the teacher may take the opposite position and do too much for him, thinking that he is incapable of putting on his own coat, walking by himself, picking up dropped objects.

Ideally, of course, the teacher will let him function just as any other child. He will not lower his standards for the student. He will expect him to work to the best of his ability. The only factor he has to consider is that the child sees with other senses than his eyes. He sees by feeling with his hands, listening with his ears.

She is Betsy, child with no useful sight.

The regular classroom teacher will undoubtedly have questions about how the child will read and write, and he naturally cannot be expected to teach the student braille. Most school systems that educate blind children hire a specially trained person to work with skills, such as reading and writing braille, mobility, and in acquiring special books, equipment and materials. This teacher may be permanently located in a school or he may travel to various schools. In either case, however, his major objective is to be of assistance to the child and to the regular teacher in the acquisition of an education of excellence.

He has conferences with the regular teacher about the child's needs and his progress. He brailles tests and written work the student will be using; he offers reassurances to the classroom teacher and answers any questions arising about the best way in which to handle certain teaching techniques for this child. For example, if the teacher is a chalkboard user, he might wonder how he can continue to be one since this child cannot see. The special teacher may suggest continued use of the chalkboard, but with assurance of an oral coverage of the work. Perhaps one of the faster students could be available to reread from the board to the blind child, should it be necessary.

The teacher may have some qualms about using words such as "see" and "look." The special teacher will reassure the classroom instructor that this child will use them also. He does see and look!

For expedience, the teacher may find himself doing some things the child could do for himself. Or he may have another help when the student could go alone. The special teacher will be working with this child on mobility skills, teaching him how to use certain techniques in travel, and he must be given an opportunity to use what he learns. Of course, there are times when he will walk with a guide, and in these cases, be certain that he holds the guide's arm rather than the other way around.

• From the first day in the classroom, the child with impaired vision should be oriented to his surroundings. Let him walk around the room, starting at the door, looking at objects along the walls, being told what the objects are and for what they are used. He will get an idea of the size of the room, how things are arranged, and will know what is where. He should be given practice on getting to his desk from the door, getting from his desk to the teacher's desk, to the trash can, to the water fountain in the hall, to the principal's office. He will watch for clues along the way, using them in the future for better mobility.

• Also from the first day, orient him to the voices and location of his classmates. It is advisable to maintain a permanent seating arrangement for everyone, at least until he knows his friends' voices. They may want to help him too much, so it is important to determine when the help is really needed and when it is not. Of course, this child wants to run and play with friends, so not all hand-in-hand travel should be discouraged.

• The totally blind child sometimes has unusual mannerisms, such as rocking back and forth, or sticking his fingers in his eyes. The recent trend is to let him be aware of what he is doing, and try to discourage it. But don't nag, or he may develop worse habits.

• He may have fears about doing all that is demanded of him, so, just as with any other child, give him praise when deserved, encouragement often. Be realistic about your demands, but don't let him get by with a minimum of effort.

• When teaching new concepts to the class, try whenever possible to give

The visually handicapped child "sees" and "looks" by actual contact with real things.

actual experiences to them. The child who cannot see a dog, for example, may have no idea what one really looks like. But if he can look at a dog, feel his fur, his ears, his tail, then the dog becomes a meaningful concept for him. If the actual experience is not possible, then an exact and vivid description is the next best thing. It is advisable to make certain this child does understand the new concept before going on to another. Often he may verbalize beautifully, but in reality, he is merely parroting what he thinks you want him to say.

The special teacher will, of course, be of much assistance concerning particulars, but here is a brief discussion of specific subjects.

Arithmetic

The concepts of size, weight, height, distance, can be taught with experiences. Compare different objects such as buttons, spools, beads. Look at the different heights of classmates. Count the number of steps needed to go to various destinations. For working problems, the blind child can use an abacus for calculating and recording answers. Or a peg board can be a method of putting down a numerical solution. The teacher can learn, with very little difficulty, the basic numbers in braille (0–9) and can check his paper right along with the others or have the special teacher interpret the braille into print.

Spelling

For written work in class, the child can do his work on his writer, and then a student who is both fast and accurate can write in print what he says he has written in braille. (Mother and Dad can do this with homework too. The child can tell them the answer, and they can write it for him. Later he can write the answer himself, with the use of a typewriter.) Honesty, of course, is a definite requirement!

Physical Education

Our visually impaired youngster needs as much exercise and play activity as anyone else, so unless he has written permission from his doctor not to participate, he should be in gym classes, too. He can learn to skip, to hop, to jump, to do exercises. He can play games. A ball with a bell inside is useful, but if not available, his playmates can tell him when the ball is coming his way, from which direction. And they can clap hands, individually, to indicate their positions. In running games, he can run with a partner until he gets the feel of the area, and has confidence in where he is to run.

Arts and Crafts

He can make the same things the others make. Show him what his goal is. Describe the materials used. He can learn to cut with scissors, to paste and to color with crayolas. He should be made aware of the various colors even if he cannot see them: he can learn to associate green with grass, blue with the sky, etc. He can even learn to discriminate between the various crayolas by having them marked in some distinguishing way. All the reds could be in one type of container, the yellows, in another. Or certain notching can be done on his own set.

Pictures can be outlined with hardened glue. Too much detail should be avoided or the picture could be a meaningless conglomeration of lines. Use sandpaper and other textures to indicate different things.

Social Studies

Raised maps, globes and Atlases with raised lines are available. *My Weekly Reader* is printed in braille, too.

Reading

Most reading books are available in braille. If workbooks are not available, the special teacher will be of assistance in brailling the work. The child can be put in an appropriate reading group comparable to his own skills. For outside reading, there are many books in braille and he can obtain them. Talking books (books on record) are on hand from his regional division of the Library of Congress.

For the child who has some useful vision, large print books are available but he can often read regular print, though slowly, by getting right up on the page, or by using a low-vision aid, such as a magnifying glass. Let him use these methods. The major disadvantage is the speed, or lack of it, involved.

Writing

For the totally blind child, a braille writer is the easiest means of writing. It is similar to a typewriter, with six keys, corresponding to the six dots of which all braille characters and letters are made. A special type of paper is used, heavier than regular paper. The dots are raised on the paper when the keys required to form each letter are pressed. He can read what he has written with a minimum of effort. A more portable writing instrument is the pocket guide and stylus. The process is a little more complicated, as the dots are pushed downward with the stylus. In order to read what is formed, the words are written from right to left. The paper must be turned over to read the words from left to right.

Pencil writing is possible for the blind child, though the task is often arduous, and sometimes illegible. He should be taught to write his own name and how to hold the pencil. There are aids for such writing but this is another of the skills the special teacher will teach him.

Teaching a child with visual impairment can be accomplished with ease, with a few changes in technique, and with no special strain. The special teacher wants to be of assistance, both with technical aspects and with answers and suggestions for the teacher. A good relationship between teacher, child and special teacher can enable everyone to achieve the goal of an education of excellence.

For additional information about the visually impaired, contact:

American Foundation for the Blind
15 West 16th Street
New York, New York 10011

The American Printing House for the Blind
1839 Frankfort Avenue
Louisville, Kentucky 40206
(*Publishers of braille materials, appliances, aids.
Catalog available.*)

Library of Congress, Division for the Blind
and Physically Handicapped
1291 Taylor Street NW
Washington, D.C. 20542
(*Supply braille books, talking books. Catalog
available. Also furnish addresses of Regional
Divisions.*

Association for the Education of the Visually
Handicapped
711 Fourteenth Street NW
Washington, D.C. 20005

*A publication offering specific suggestions and
ideas on teaching exceptional children is avail-
able four times a year.*
TEACHING EXCEPTIONAL CHILDREN
1201 16th Street NW
Washington, D.C. 20036
(*Present fee is $5.00 for subscriptions within the
USA*)

Another publication available is a pamphlet entitled
THE VISUALLY HANDICAPPED CHILD
AT HOME AND SCHOOL
John W. Jones, U.S. Department of Health,
Education and Welfare

*For an understanding of what the blind child faces
and how he can lead a near normal life, an un-
usual and beautifully written book is:*
AND THERE WAS LIGHT
Jaques Lusseyran
Little, Brown and Company
Boston
1963

6

Creativity and Communication: An Approach to Elementary School Language Arts

Evelyn Gray Harris

ABOUT THE AUTHOR

Evelyn Harris received the Bachelor of Science in Elementary Education degree from Longwood College in Farmville, Virginia. She has taught the sixth grade for several years and is presently with the Hampton, Virginia school system. Mrs. Harris was director of playground activities in Portsmouth, Virginia for three years. During the summer of 1968 she helped to compile a teaching guide for the Hampton schools.

Have you seen the confused and frustrated faces of children who say, "No—I meant . . .", "You didn't understand it.", "Don't make me read it—it's silly." For these youngsters the English language is a puzzle: a maze of grammar rules and punctuation marks.

Creative writing is more than fairy tales and short stories. When organized and presented as a *total* program of language arts, it makes language serve a useful purpose in all daily activities—no matter what the subject matter, grade level or socio-economic conditions of an area. Equally as important, it gives the child confidence in *his* manner of expressing personal feelings, opinions or knowledge of facts.

The following program in language arts will help a child develop his own style in speaking and writing as he learns the organizational and structural skills which allow him to state his ideas effectively.

Adapt these ideas to your grade level. Some of the activities may be too complex for primary students but their basic aims may be shared by any age.

The class may be grouped by specific interests and needs:

The Clarity Group—Children with real difficulty in forming sentences and choosing words to express their ideas.

The Disciplined Group—The "average" children who need special motivation to fire them. Practice in organizing thoughts and elaboration of ideas is stressed.

The Creative Group—Children who are naturally good writers and are interested in almost everything. They learn to develop style and can do many colorful, dramatic and independent things —challenging and enjoying the work of their group mates.

THE ESSAY

Communication Goals

- Learning to describe people, places, objects, ideas, situations and feelings.
- Learning to read and interpret what others have written or said.
- Expressing personal opinions convincingly because they are based on facts and observations.

Writing Skills

- Writing sensible sentences.
- Building a paragraph.
- Using transition sentences between paragraphs.
- Putting paragraphs in best order.
- Beginning a paper or speech so as to capture interest, and making a firm summary statement at the end.

Activities

- Descriptions
    1. Motivate interest in sentences by reading humorous sentences which are funny because—
        ✔ they are incomplete.
        ✔ they have modifiers in the wrong place,
        ✔ they use inappropriate words to describe.
    2. Have children present skits or cartoons illustrating confused sentences.

If you want to hit the coach, Mr. Lane will show you how.

Skits point out the failure to say what is meant. Children can correct such sentences as a group.

3. Have students prepare check lists for their notebooks.

Grammar   Check List
1. Are sentences sensible?
2. Are words used correctly?
3. Have I checked spellings?
4. Did I leave out necessary words?
5. Did I put in extra words?
6. Did I proof-read <u>aloud</u>, reading every word?

Content Check List
1. Do paragraphs have a strong topic sentence?
2. Did I use transition and summary sentences?
3. Does the essay begin with an especially interesting sentence?
4. Are opinions firmly supported?

Form Check List
(Do I have ---)
1. Title
2. Skipped lines
3. Indented paragraphs
4. Margins
5. Neat, clean pages
6. Name and date at the end

4. Give assignments in describing a person:
   a. Write a topic sentence which includes a few words or a phrase about each of these qualities: looks, actions, feelings.
   b. Fill in the paragraph with two sentences about each quality.
   c. Write a sentence summarizing your reactions to this person.
5. Give assignments in describing a scene—a park, a house, a fire— using knowledge of good paragraph structure:
   a. Begin with an interesting topic sentence.
   b. Build with facts.
   c. Top off with summary.

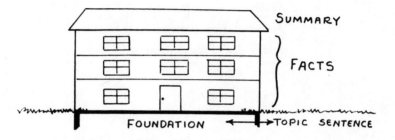

6. Give assignments in relating experiences:
   a. Ask children to describe a trip or an exciting experience.
   b. Divide the story into three sections:

THE BROTHER HUNT

   I. David Is Discovered Missing

   II. The Hunt

   III. Found!

   c. Write a paragraph about each section. At the ends of parts I and II, use a transition sentence which will lead to the next part and will keep the story interesting.
   d. Make the first sentence of the essay very exciting.
   e. Make the last paragraph end the event and sum up the experience.
7. Give assignments in opinions vs. fact:
   a. Ask the class, "What do you think about a 12 month school year?"
      • See how many can give you good reasons for their feelings which were so readily expressed!

  b. Stress the importance of being able to back up opinions with
     fact and to be polite and tactful when expressing opinions.
  c. Assign several controversial topics of immediate interest to
     the children. Remind them to back up their opinions with
     facts.

WEEKLY WRITING ASSIGNMENTS

Insist that a written paper be planned throughout the week.

  Monday—Statement of topic

  Tuesday—Outline of paragraphs

  Wednesday—Rough copy

  Thursday—Final proofing by check lists

  Friday—Inked copy turned in

THE SHORT STORY

Creative Communication Skill

- Learning to express feelings and ideas through interesting and well-
  organized fictional events which are based on things that could happen
  in our everyday world or in another world.

Writing Skills

- Choosing colorful, descriptive and action words to form a picture in the
  reader's mind.
- Learning to punctuate and paragraph dialogue.

Literary Appreciation

- Awareness of good stories which develop character, setting, events.
  climax and meaning.

Activities

  1. Choose several stories which will appeal to your group. Read and
     discuss—what made them interesting?
  2. Prepare a poster with the common dialogue rules.

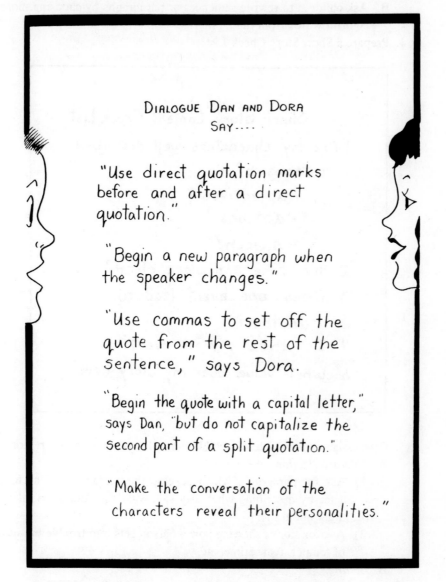

DIALOGUE DAN AND DORA
SAY····

"Use direct quotation marks before and after a direct quotation."

"Begin a new paragraph when the speaker changes."

"Use commas to set off the quote from the rest of the sentence," says Dora.

"Begin the quote with a capital letter," says Dan, "but do not capitalize the second part of a split quotation."

"Make the conversation of the characters reveal their personalities."

A. Write a running conversation on the board with no punctuation or paragraphing.
B. Following the rules for punctuation, ask children to act out the dialogue.
C. On the other side of the board punctuate each paragraph. Have the children give the rule for each change.
3. Collect descriptive and action words.
A. Teach the use of dictionaries and a simple thesaurus.

B. Ask children to rewrite sentences or paragraphs by choosing more colorful words from the thesaurus.

4. Prepare a Short Story Check List:

Short Story Content Check List

1. Are my characters well-described in terms of –
   - adjectives ?
   - actions ?
   - speech ?
2. Are time and place clear?
3. Does one event lead to another?
4. Is there a main event?
5. What value does my story have?

5. Give assignments which help children develop parts of the short story:
   A. *Characterization*
      1) Ask for paragraphs which develop the personality of a character by describing what they say, what they do, what others think about them.
      2) Ask for stories showing how a person gets into trouble because of temper, fear, crime, etc.
   B. *Setting*
      1) Ask for paragraphs which make time and place clear
         a) *Directly*—by stating it
         b) *Indirectly*—by what the characters do, say, wear.
   C. *Events*
      1) Ask for a list of the events which will occur in the story.
      2) Ask children to star the event which will be most exciting.
   D. *Meaning, Moral, Lesson*
      1) Read several stories to the class. Ask them to state the point

of each story—its moral, meaning, lesson. Discuss. Compare.
2) Read their stories to the class. Ask for the same statement of meaning, moral or lesson. Discuss. Compare.

SHORT STORY WRITING ASSIGNMENT

Insist that the story be planned throughout the week.

Monday—Statement of topic and theme

Tuesday—Characterization, setting, outline of events

Wednesday—Rough copy

Thursday—Final proofing

Friday—Inked copy turned in

The day the stories are returned:

1. Discuss common errors in grammar, content, development and format.

2. Ask children to copy the corrected story, illustrate and save for short story booklets.

MEET —

Composed Carol

• WELL ORGANIZED
• GRAMMATICAL
• NEAT
• INTERESTING

DOES YOUR COMPOSITION HAVE THESE QUALITIES?

6. *Short Story Booklets*

When this unit of work is completed, the copies and illustrated stories are compiled into individual short story booklets with:

> Cover
> Title page
> Dedication
> Introduction
> Table of contents
> List of illustrations
> Stories
> Summary
> Blank pages

The booklets may be displayed and read by others.

- The booklets may be displayed and read by others. With library card pockets pasted on the back cover, they might be treated as library editions and checked out by different class members.
- If each child chooses what he believes to be his best story, it can be copied into a class anthology.

With library card pockets pasted on the back cover, the booklets are treated as library editions and checked out by different class members.

7. *The Author's Club*

Each week different students are awarded membership in the Author's Club on the basis of their stories. The stories are chosen by the teacher or the children. The author of the stories remain unknown until the vote is taken.

Club members receive certificates and have their names posted on a special bulletin board.

Prize-winning stories go into a special anthology and are loaned to the school library.

PLAY WRITING

Lead directly from the writing of short stories to the writing of plays. Take the best of the short stories they have created and try some of these activities:

1. Make three stories into one act plays.
    a. List scenes.
    b. List characters in each play.
    c. Outline events of scenes.
    d. Write dialogue and stage directions.
    e. Assign props and scenery chairmen.
    f. Decide on simple costumes.
    g. Practice and present.
2. Turn different stories into puppet shows.
3. Take different characters and try to dress and act as they do in the story. Is it difficult to do? Does the story need stronger descriptive material?
4. Concentrate on presenting specific scenes from a story. Is it difficult to do? How could action be improved?

TELLING A STORY

Story telling can also develop naturally from the students' short stories.
1. Have students dress as an old-timer spinning a sea yarn, a witch reviewing her favorite hair-raising experience, an old man or woman recounting earlier days.
2. Ask students to use a check list as they prepare and present a story-telling assignment:

Story Teller Check List

1. Was my story appropriate for the age of the audience?

2. Did I use expression of face and voice?

3. Were the events of my story well-planned?

4. Was my voice loud and clear?

5. Did I use simple props or costumes to make the story more interesting?

CLASSROOM PUBLICATIONS

When the children have been exposed to both the expository writing skills of the essay and the structure of the short story, a classroom newspaper and magazine might be printed.

Through such publications children will see—
- ✔ The importance of meeting deadlines in all work
- ✔ The real need for proofreading
- ✔ The importance of planning ahead

1. Ask children to bring newspapers to school. Examine and discuss their main parts.
2. Decide what type of material their classroom reporters could prepare for each part:

   News—class, school, city, state, national, international.

   Editorials—controversial school activity

   Features—human interest—class member, teacher, staff member

   Sports—class, school, city, national, international

   Amusements—movies, television, top songs, cartoons, riddles, "Dear Minnie Manners" column

   Advertisements—jobs wanted, articles wanted, personals, vital statistics

3. Have each child write a news, feature or sport article, a letter to the editor and something for the amusement or ad page.
4. Organize a staff:

   a. Editor-in-chief

   b. Five section editors

   c. Publisher (teacher)

5. Choose a name and seal for the paper.
6. Prepare a file for ideas, finished articles, proofed articles and copies of the printed paper.

Each child should write one article each time in the News, Feature or Sports area. Some won't be used but an effort to balance authorship of printed articles should be made.

Children who finish their articles should consult with the Amusement and Advertising editors who will have planned their pages and will need help filling them in.

There is a great deal of work in this unit and children will need time to plan, interview, write, proof, assemble, lay-out and print. The project

Reporters learn the importance of meeting deadlines as they arrange for interviews, then organize notes and write their articles.

should continue throughout the year even though the paper may be published only once a month.

Correlated with the newspaper work and the story-writing projects, there might be a magazine published every two months. It could contain art work (lines and shading only), short stories, poetry and book reviews.

THE AUTOBIOGRAPHY

Begin a unit on autobiographies by reading to the class a well-done biography of a person who interests them. Explain how biographies and autobiographies differ.

Prepare a schedule for the writing of their autobiographies.

Ask for two chapters a week. Require rough copies and outlines of paragraph contents.

Children may interview their relatives for the events which happened before they can remember.

SCHEDULE FOR AUTOBIOGRAPHY

A. Chapters

    1.   Vital Statistics of Birth

    2.   Pre-school Mmeories

    3.   Parent Characterization

    4.   Brothers and Sisters

        (If none, tell if you like
        being an only child.)

    5.   Favorite "Other Relative".

    6.   Best Friends Through the Ages

    7.   Places Lived

    8.   An Admired Adult

    9.   Pets

        (If none, would you like
        having one?)

    10.   Hobbies and Liesure Time

    11.   Most Exciting - or Most Frightening
        Experience

    12.   Happiest Moments

    13.   Feelings About School

    14.   Plans For the Future

B. Dates Due

    1.   _____

    2.   _____

    3.   _____

    4.   _____

When the chapters are finished and illustrated and photos included, stress originality of cover, dedication and general presentation. The children will love sharing their booklets and voting for the best-done booklet or most interesting life.

To add interest to this project, children might bring baby pictures which are mounted, unidentified and numbered. The child identifying the greatest number of classmates may be awarded a small prize.

Also, amusing or exciting parts of different autobiographies may be read and the children allowed to guess to whom they refer.

WRITING POETRY

The music of words—poetry may be rhymed or not—but, in any case, it is the most personal of literary expression. It need not have complete sentences or complete thoughts.

The magic of poetry is in its sound, its feeling or mood, and its rhythm. The aims of the poetry unit include:

- Appreciation of poetry as a literary form
- Capitalization and punctuation in poetry
- Practice in writing forms of
  - (1) limerick
  - (2) lyric
  - (3) narrative
  - (4) ballad
  - (5) haiku
  - (6) free verse
- Relating poetry to music, especially that with lyric and ballad characteristics.

The unit may begin with the reading of different types of poems. Keep them brief, and let the children write a simple statement telling what they did or did not like about number 1 or number 2, etc.

Play a record of lyric and ballad type music, and add those to your survey.

Make a study of the responses and read the poems which were not enjoyed with comments about them.

Pass out mimeographed copies of some poems, or use some in reading or song books. Have as many poetry anthologies in the room as possible.

Ask children to note:

Capitalization of the first word of a line
Method of indenting
Punctuation
Rhyming of words
Pattern of line and syllables

1. The Limerick

Select several to read and discuss. Write them on the board. Practice writing a few on the spur of the moment. Assign 2 or 3 per child. When limericks are returned and shared, have them copied and illustrated. Have each child keep one or two for his poetry booklet.

2. The Lyric

Copy, illustrate and choose lyric poems from anthologies or song books. Have children make a list of words describing a scene or person. Beside them list homonyms. Build a class lyric poem from these lists.

Poetry is personal.

3. The Narrative

Read "The Wreck of the Hesperus," "The Highwayman," "The Midnight Ride of Paul Revere." Choose a theme based on history and have the children outline the events which could be included in the verses.

Try choral reading and acting out scenes as individual poems are read.

4. The Ballad

This is an excellent chance to relate the current popularity of folk and "country" music. There are many books available giving words, simple chording and the history of the songs.

Studying the words and origins of a few old favorites will help the children understand more about people from other sections of our country as well as about foreign ancestries.

Have the children write ballads based on their lives or events in the world today. Show how this helps people of the future.

5. Haiku

This form of poetry is refreshing. Of Japanese origin, it is a very short poem made of seventeen syllables contained in three lines generally of 5, 7, 5 syllables.

Because it lacks length, it has two important poetic qualities:
- it is fresh.
- it leaves much to the imagination of the reader.

Three delightful references have been published by the Peter Pauper Press:

Japanese Haiku
The Four Seasons
Cherry Blossoms

Discuss the use of words to show pictures.

A hidden idea in the mind of the child should be created in his poem— or a descriptive poem may be written.

6. Free Verse

The beat and position of words is stressed here. There may be no regularity of rhythm or rhyme and there are seldom complete sentences. The author may have a one word line to stress a word.

Choose an emotion from a list of love, joy, surprise, hate, envy, fear. Ask the children to do a free verse poem describing their feeling.

Ask them to begin a new line at every pause which is in their minds and to capitalize accordingly. Ask them to use punctuation to accentuate feeling.

A poetry program based on old favorites and original class poems may be given with some acting out of poems, choral reading and singing of songs included.

THE RESEARCH PAPER

In elementary school situations the research paper depends on a good school library, a classroom sharing center made up of books brought by children, and a genuine interest in the chosen topic.

Communication Goals

- Learning to make use of all resources available and to recognize unusual resources.
- Learning to use facts from several sources and to draw conclusions in one's own words.
- Learning to outline properly.
- Acquiring letter writing skills.

Activities

1. Ask the children to think of one thing in which they are really interested and would like to know more about. (The topics may range from motorcycles to hairdos, but it must be their own choice.)

2. When the topic is approved and you have suggested places to locate information, show the children how to make a simple reference list.

3. Explain that the reference list will give direction to their research and will grow throughout the unit. Card catalogues, indexes, tables of contents, business firms and fellow students may be included in the search.

Each sheet of references should include:

Name of reference (Key)—Date published—volume and pages.

The key may include:

(E)	encyclopedia
(N)	newspaper
(M)	magazine
(I)	interview
(NF)	other non-fiction
(A)	atlas
(P)	pamphlet

This exploring of resources can take the first week while the children learn or review the form and content of letters requesting full information. Keep government agencies in mind. They are most helpful, and this is one way to show the children that their country is interested in them.

Plan as many resource periods as you can, and make an effort to find information and bring it to the class reference shelf. Your interest will be rewarded!

A list of topics and the students' names can be posted so that class members may help each other find resources.

When five or six references have been examined, an outline of chapters should be listed with Roman numerals. Capital letters can represent subheads or paragraphs, and numerals represent important facts to be included in each paragraph. The facts will be filled in as notetaking progresses, but planning of chapters and subheads can be done after initial research and planning.

Notetaking may work out better on sheets of paper than on note cards. At any rate, insist on:

- using *one reference* per page
- only one chapter per page
- use one side of the paper

Explain how this makes chapter planning easier since notes of one type may be shuffled to get good order in paragraphs.

Each sheet:

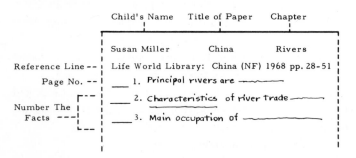

Encourage writing notes in the child's own words. Footnoting is confusing, but quotation marks may be used for copied material, so the children become accustomed to giving proper credit to the ideas of others.

Keep a folder of the children's outlines. Tell them when each chapter is due:

- Monday and Tuesday may be research days.
- Notes and chapter outlines are due on Wednesdays.

- The final chapter is due on Friday.
- The outlines are corrected by chapters and returned weekly to be copied for the final booklet. Encourage the children to have special work folders to keep:
  - all notes
  - general and chapter outlines
  - uncopied chapters
  - the growing reference list
  - pamphlets and pictures
  - the copied chapters which are ready for the booklet.
    Include in the final booklet:

    cover
    title page
    dedication
    table of contents
    list of photos and illustrations
    chapters
    summary
    appendix

This type of language arts program will result in better writers, speakers, and thinkers who know how to arrange their thoughts in an orderly and interesting way. Your students will have been introduced to basic literary forms, have heard good literature and organized and shared their own. They will be proud of their part in the growing class library and of their ability to find information, and to channel their feelings, ideas and opinions. They will have the skills necessary to be understood by others. Thus, a varied and lively English program serves a vital purpose as it shows the beauties of a word well-said.

For brilliant insight into the teaching of English and creative writing—
David Holbrook's
- ENGLISH FOR MATURITY
  New York: Cambridge University Press, 1962
- ENGLISH FOR THE REJECTED
  New York: Cambridge University Press, 1964
- THE SECRET PLACES
  Tuscaloosa: University of Alabama Press, 1965
- THE EXPLORING MIND
  New York: Cambridge University Press, 1967

7

A Non-Reader Begins to Read

Cynthia W. Craig

ABOUT THE AUTHOR

Cynthia Craig holds the Bachelor of Arts degree from Florida State University and the Master of Arts from the University of Florida. She is certified in Administration and Supervision, Guidance, English, Elementary Education, Reading and Sociology. She teaches the course "Reading Resources for Elementary Children" for St. Johns River Junior College. Mrs. Craig has taught in the public schools for 19 years, including two years with the Homebound Program for elementary children. She is presently a tutoring clinician with the Duval County Reading Laboratory in Jacksonville, Florida.

James Johns, ten years old, of normal or average intelligence, was socially promoted to a fourth grade classroom. There seemed no ready-made program that would fit James. He was a severely handicapped reader—a non-reader—and this chapter shows some of the material which helped him begin to read. He not only began to read, he began to find it a pleasant and rewarding experience.

Although James's problems were extreme, the activities and games which were developed to help him can be adapted for use with individuals or groups working in the classroom.

Learning the Individual Letters

As each letter of the alphabet was presented, it was given a personality, a characterization. While the letter was discussed, its picture was drawn

71

on the board and later transferred to permanent alphabet cards.

r is a loudmouth
r is never quiet
r wants to be heard

p is a pig
p is powerful
p is noisy and loud

Next a group of pictures was presented illustrating the particular letter:
rug, rose, rake
pig, puppy, pan

James looked at them, pronounced them, looked in a mirror as he said
them. This procedure was continued through each of the 26 letters.

The Sand Tray and Sand Cards

A teacher can waste a great deal of time cutting out kinesthetic materials from sandpaper. If she will gather a pack of 3″ x 5″ file cards, a magic marker, bottle of Elmer's glue and some plain sand or pretty colored silicant from the Aquarium Corner of the dime store, she is ready to prepare very effective kinesthetic tools.

Each lesson with James was begun with the letter sand cards. (It is important to do this work with the child. If you prepare the materials ahead of time, they do not have the same meaning. When the child does it with you, the knowledge gained is his.)

They did not say the letters, they said the word. They wrote it, traced it, played with it many, many times in the sand tray (a baking pan from the dime store). Then they made the card.

1. The letters were written first with black magic marker on a 3″ x 5″ file card, then traced over with Elmer's glue.

2. Next James placed the card in the tray and piled the sand and silicant over it.
3. When the card was removed, the rough raised form of the word remained. (It takes only a minute for the glue to dry so the card can be used.)
4. Two cards were made—one for James to take home and one for his folder at school.
5. At first a key picture was pasted on the back of the cards so James could associate one word with each letter.

The cards were placed in front of James, one at a time, at the beginning of each lesson. The teacher was careful not to let him miss more than one or two a day. She held the others back after he had made two mistakes. Games for that lesson were based on the letter or letters he missed.

An excellent chapter on the kinesthetic method can be found in Grace Fernauld's *Remedial Techniques in Basic School Subjects,* McGraw-Hill, 1943.

Beginning Sounds

Walk through the house, stroll through the dime store. Collect small bottles, lace, a watch, figurines, models, utensils—anything that has a beginning letter and can be kept in a box! James was asked to sort materials of this type into small paper trays or boxes, showing that he could identify the beginning sounds. A teacher might concentrate on just a few consonants, a few vowels—or the entire alphabet.

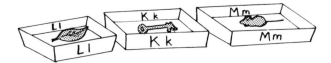

Beginning and Ending Consonants

Small card holders were prepared for each consonant by taping cardboard with Mystic tape. Pictures of objects were cut from magazines and merchandizing catalogs and mounted on 3″ x 5″ cards. James identified the beginning (or ending) consonant and placed the card in its proper pocket.

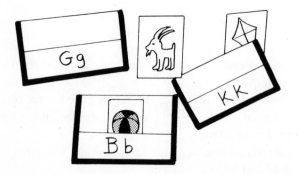

Games

Any number of "games" can be designed to interest children in calling off letters, sounds and words.

BOUNCE THE BLOCKS

Small blocks were made by placing masking tape on one inch wooden cubes, then writing letters on the tape with magic marker. Only two letters were placed on each block. The game involved tossing the cubes and naming the letters as they fell.

GOING FISHING

Fish were cut from oak-tag and different words or sounds written across them. A ½" piece of strip magnet was attached to the back of each fish. The fishing pole—a branch with a magnet for the hook—was used to catch the fish. James pronounced the sounds or words as he caught his fish.

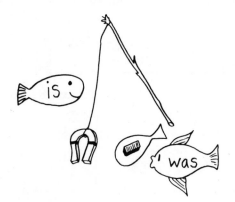

LET'S FLY A KITE

Kite shapes were fished out by a magnet on a string. James pronounced the words or sounds written on the face of the kites.

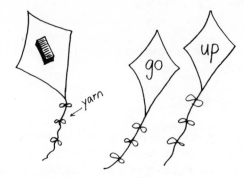

**MOVE THE BEE—GIVE THE DOG A BONE—
HELP KITTY FIND HER MILK**

Drawings were made on desk size sheets of oak-tag. Rectangles were marked off to give James a spot to place his word cards. As he called off popper cards, flash cards, word cards of any kind, he advanced the bee (or dog or cat) toward its goal.

Any sort of drawing can be used—soldiers moving toward a fort, picnickers crossing a stream, pirates sailing toward an island, dinosaurs moving to a swamp, etc.

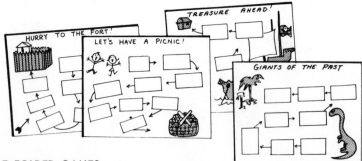

FILE FOLDER GAMES

Countless numbers of games were prepared on the inside of manila file folders. To make these, rule off the edges of the folder. Indicate in the center and on the top filing tab which sound, phonogram or type of word is being emphasized. Clip an envelope to the folder to hold the instruction slips. The *start* and *stop* blocks might be indicated with a bright color. Pennies, rocks or bingo pieces can be used as markers.

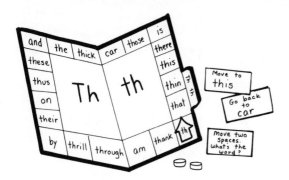

ALPHABET BINGO

On chipboard, oak-tag or cardboard the teacher ruled off squares and printed different letters of the alphabet. James picked up picture cards or toys and identified their beginning (or ending) sounds. He placed a marker on his bingo card if it had the matching sound.

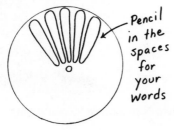

The Controlled Reader

Educational Development Laboratories makes Flash-X—a controlled reader for one student. The teacher bought the plain cards to make word wheels for James. (If you buy the plain cards, be sure to circle the openings in pencil before printing your words so they will be properly centered when they are flashed in the reader.)

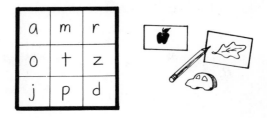

Pencil in the spaces for your words

Experience Charts

Experience stories have been used for many years by teachers—so much so that it is surprising when a teacher is heard to remark, "I've made many experience charts with children but I never knew what to do with them after they were written." For James, they were the vehicle by which he could begin to read.

On the day that James learned the word "boy," the teacher wrote:

James is a boy.

She read it to him, then asked him to read it to her. He said, "I is a boy." She wrote his sentence. Now he could see in print the words he had *said* together with the sentence he had been asked to *read*:

James is a boy.

I is a boy.

No issue was made of the correct form of speech at this point.

Three weeks from the beginning of school, James dictated his first story:

Daddy was in the Navy.

He was on a big boat.

He was on a fighting boat.

While James watched, the teacher placed the words of his story on a large wheel (diameter of seventeen inches).

He was pleased to see his words in a game he could play.

Next, word and phrase cards were made so that he could match the cards with his story's words-and-phrases to those on the chart. As he searched the story in order to match the cards, he became more fluent in reading the material. He also reconstructed the story on his desk with these cards.

Other games were prepared to help him recognize the words in isolation and to keep his interest alive.

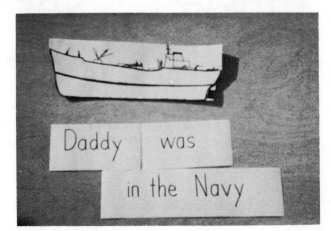

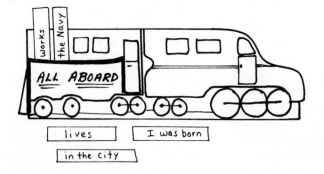

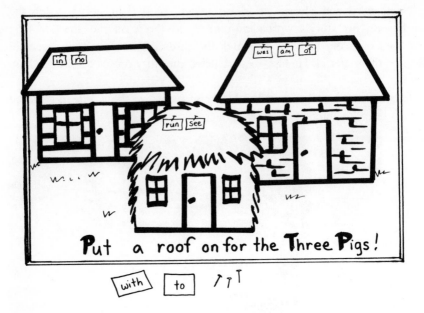

Each day James read his dictated story and played a game using its words and phrases. The teacher had to be careful that James did not lose interest through failure to read his own stories and words. It would seem that he might tire of using the same materials but success in reading was so new to him that he thoroughly enjoyed it.

Some of his stories were fun as a sharing experience but were too complex to be used as his reading lesson. These were put away for future work although some of the words were added to his working vocabulary.

Charts

The little word "at" had been used early in the year. When James learned the word "hat," an "at" chart was prepared:
Word and phrase cards were made to match the words and phrases on his chart. James also found that he could combine these into nonsense sentences. He laughed when he wrote "Daddy sat on a hat."

From the chart and cards, he progressed to an "at" tachistoscope.

Filing the Dictated Stories

The teacher used inexpensive chipboard to prepare file folders for James's and other children's stories. They were made the same size as the chart paper on which the stories were recorded. The left and bottom sides were bound with Mystic tape.

Sequence Cards

Illustrations were cut from advertisements in magazines, from discarded books, from bulletins and flyers—anything which showed a sequence of events. They were mounted on oak-tag or file cards and filed in envelopes. James arranged the pictures in proper sequence and told what happened— orally or in written sentences.

Four Size Word Cards

As James began to learn words, they were placed on vocabulary cards—on different sizes and colors of paper and in four different letter sizes to help insure that the words would be recognized wherever he found them.

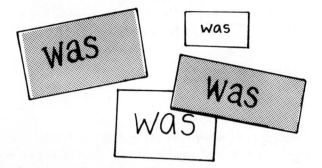

Vocabulary Reference Books

The teacher, James, and other children took pictures from catalogs, from canned goods labels, from magazines and advertisements. These were mounted in booklets which could be added to. They were categorized in many ways:

FOODS	A WORDS	JEWELRY
FRUITS	B WORDS	ANIMALS
MACHINES	CH WORDS	VEHICLES

FURNITURE   CITY LIFE   POWER EQUIPMENT

EMOTIONS   FARM LIFE   PEOPLE

All the children brought materials throughout the year to add to these booklets.

Using Materials Again and Again

Covers were made to protect special testing sheets, work sheets and puzzles that the teacher wished to mark on and use again. Two sheets of acetate, bound on the left and bottom sides with Mystic tape, make it easy to slip material in and out. A grease marking pencil makes the best writing instrument. (If you wish to use pages from a workbook in which the correct answers have been circled, circle all the responses before inserting the sheet in the acetate folder.)

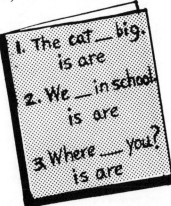

Circulating Extra Reading Material

The teacher attached a library pocket card to the front of magazines, single stories (sealed in acetate) and extra copies of discarded books which had been salvaged from the library and book depository. The children signed out for these materials on 3″ x 5″ cards, took them home or kept them at their desks for use in spare moments.

Book Jacket Puzzles

To help encourage interest in reading, the teacher mounted book jackets on heavy cardboard and cut them into puzzles. A frame was prepared by cutting the center out of one piece of corrugated cardboard and gluing the border to a second piece the same size. The outlines of the puzzle pieces were marked on the frame as a guide for the children to follow.

The books were handy for reading when the puzzles were completed!

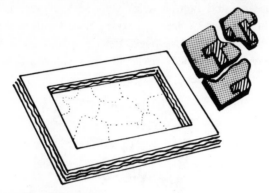

Progress Report

From alphabet cards and sand trays through experience charts and games, James came from a pre-readiness program to a pre-primer level in three and one-half months' time. By June he was reading primer level books —pleased and proud of himself and anxious to get on with the business of reading.

8

The Library: Motivating Through Displays

Claire Kiker

ABOUT THE AUTHOR

Claire Kiker received her Bachelor of Arts and Master of Science degrees from Florida State University. She has conducted the summer reading program for the Ferry Pass School in Pensacola, Florida and is presently its full-time librarian. Since December, 1968, she has been librarian for the Cooperative Masters Degree Program in Aeronautical Systems with the University of West Florida and the Naval Air Training Command.

A student quite often comes to the library with no idea of what he really wants to read. Bulletin boards and displays can trigger a response and lead him down the path to enjoyable reading.

• A bulletin board at the entrance of a library or classroom confronts the child immediately. The simplest ideas are most effective here since a glance is often all the students can afford to give the board. That glance is followed-up through another display. For example, the board might post the scores of a weekend football game over exciting action pictures. In another section of the room a collection of football stories could be pulled and highlighted with a football, megaphone, pennant or crepe paper streamers.

• Pegboards are an extremely versatile way to display. They are easily moved, can be used as partitions and lend themselves well to different types of exhibits; flat, 3-D, shelved, etc.

• Pegboards also make it possible to create a quiet corner where readers will not be disturbed or distracted. Book jackets and book reviews by student critics can be displayed in these corners. The critiques might carry a by-line and the students' photographs to capture attention. (Our library has a polaroid for "promotional" purposes!) Books reviewed by the students should be readily available—often hung on pegboard book racks by the review.

● Pegboards can be put on wheels. A school librarian or classroom teachers can prepare several displays to circulate around the school. Books or book lists accompany the material and make it easy for the children to follow up a spark of interest.

● An exhibit case can do a great deal to push books. Exhibits can be shown for a week in the library, hall or classroom. Anyone in school is eligible to display his work or collection. Books relating to the exhibit can be subtly displayed nearby. The supply is usually exhausted long before the exhibit is changed.

● Children seem to think that teachers don't communicate with each other and are amazed when the library is pushing poetry at the same time they are studying poetry in their classrooms. Cooperation between class and library makes doubly sure that children have complete exposure to all the material which is available in a teacher's unit.

● It is best to use subjects of real interest to the children. A "Welcome to Spring" board featuring odes to spring might be beautiful, but as appealing to children as double homework assignments.

● Displays and exhibits should not be confined to books alone. Filmstrips, records and tapes should also be displayed and some provision made for using them. A multi-media approach does a lot to sell any theme! Pegboards can partition off listening posts or carrel space for children to work with single concept projectors, film strip previewers, tape recorders or phonographs. Small science exhibits might be set up by the students with related 8mm single concept cartridges, reference books and pamphlets available. Children appreciate the independence of gaining knowledge and handling equipment by themselves.

● Many children react strangely when directly approached to read a book. They seem to resent the interference although they still need guidance. They *will* read books that other children are reading, reasoning that they must be good. Leaving book trucks around with books to be shelved, or placing them casually on a library table insures that they will be read.

● There are many ways to get ideas for exhibits and displays:

■ *The Wilson Library Bulletin* is perhaps the best consultant for display ideas. Its bulletin boards can be adapted to almost any situation and most issues include an article on displays and exhibits.

- Keep a book of quotations handy. They are always good for ideas.
- Let your students plan displays. They are the only ones who know the "in" facts on what is popular with the children. The final product might not be as professional, but your pupils will be satisfied and you can be sure they will bring their friends to see.
- Working closely with other teachers is a good way to get ideas. You might share a bibliography of media about your current unit and ask them to share theirs with you. When completed, file the material in the library for everyone to use.
- Watch store windows, magazine and newspaper ads for ideas. The professional advertisers have done all the ground work—let them help you "sell" whatever unit, topic or concept you are teaching. Keep your notebook handy when you're shopping. Jot down ideas; make sketches; note the use of materials, colors, highlights, arrangements, slogans.
- Keep your book jackets (and all author information you can find) on file.
- Store your bulletin board supplies in a suitcase! It's easy to carry from board to board, or from display case to pegboard corner.
- Keep your eyes open for interesting and unusual materials. If you have a paper or printing company in the area, ask them to let you rummage through their scrap pile. You'll find all sorts of valuable (to you) goodies: various textured papers, interesting colors, corrugated material, framing and mounting boards, and the like.
- Visit local fabric shops and decorator shops. Ask them to save discarded materials for you: scraps, wallpaper books, color charts, etc.
- Spend some time with the *Educator's Guide to Free Materials* (Educator's Progress Service, Randolph, Wisc.), *Free and Inexpensive Learning Materials* (George Peabody College for Teachers, Nashville, Tenn.) and *Free and Inexpensive Educational Aids* (Thomas J. Pope, New York: Dover).
- Whatever your display, avoid—overcrowding, too broad a topic, too much detail, unrelated material and too-long exposure. Keep your material simple and it will not be difficult to change it frequently.

You can use just about anything and everything in the course of a year. Start collecting:

Aluminum foil	Balsa wood	Brushes
Brown paper	Colored tape	Chalk
Cardboard	Drinking straws	Crayon
Chart paper	Felt	Felt pens
Construction paper	Pipe cleaners	Flat pens

Corrugated paper	Popsicle sticks	
Crepe paper	Pre-cut letters	Charcoal
Gift wrap paper	Ribbon	Ink
Oak-tag	String	Pastels
Poster paper	Twigs	Tempera
Wall paper	Wire	Watercolor
	Yarn	
Liners	Razor blades	Fabrics
Rulers	Scissors	Styrofoam
	X-acto knives	
Book jackets		Newspapers
Striking illustrations	Bulletin board wax	Magazines
Maps	Map tacks	
	Masking tape	Advertising pieces
Buttons	Pins	Bulletins
Egg cartons	Rubber cement	Pamphlets
Golf tees	Scotchtape	
Paper cups	Staplers	
Small boxes	Stick-tax	
Tubes		

Well Worth Reading:

Coplan, Kate. *Effective Library Exhibits, Poster Ideas and Bulletin Board Techniques.* Dobbs Ferry, N.Y.: Oceana, 1962.

"Displays for the Month," *Wilson Library Bulletin.* New York: Wilson Monthly.

Materials to Encourage Vacation Reading. New York: Children's Book Council.

Mathre, L. H. *Creative Bulletin Boards.* Minneapolis: Denison, 1963.

Miller, Ray. *Bulletin Boards—High, Wide, and Handsome.* Riverside: Bruce Miller, 1961.

Pavlovic, Lora and Goodman, Elizabeth. *The Elementary School Library in Action.* West Nyack: Parker Publishing Co., Inc., 1968.

Tiedt, Iris M. *Bulletin Board Captions.* San Jose, California: Contemporary Press, 1965.

Highly Recommended:

Bowers, Melvyn K. *Easy Bulletin Boards for the School Library.* New York: Scarecrow Press, 1966.

Lee, Carver. *The Library Bulletin Board Guide.* Minneapolis, Minn.: Denison, 1965.

Linleer, Jerry Mac. *Instructional Display Boards.* Instructional Media Center, Division of Extension, The University of Texas at Austin, 1968.

Guimarin, Spencer. *Lettering Techniques.* Visual Instruction Bureau, Division of Extension, The University of Texas, 1965.

Smith, Richard E. *Local Production Techniques.* Visual Instruction Bureau, Division of Extension, The University of Texas, 1966.

Lockridge, J. Preston. *Better Bulletin Board Displays.* Visual Instruction Bureau, Division of Extension, The University of Texas, 1960.

Lockridge, J. Preston. *Educational Displays and Exhibits.* Visual Instruction Bureau, Division of Extension, The University of Texas, 1966.

9

Why Art?—

Philip P. Resnack

ABOUT THE AUTHOR

Philip Resnack holds the Bachelor of Arts and Master of Arts degrees from Wayne University in Detroit, Michigan. He has taught in the Detroit Public School system, at Peabody Teacher's College, and has given extension classes for the University of California at Los Angeles. Mr. Resnack was art supervisor of the San Bernardino City Schools and is presently the art supervisor for the Santa Monica Unified School District in Santa Monica, California. He has been an artist and educator for 22 years.

Art can stimulate the imagination and inventiveness of the student. It can increase awareness, open new doors, and extend boundaries. Through art, the student can give his experiences, his concepts, his ideas and feelings physical form, and in a variety of materials both two- and three-dimensional. This can be especially meaningful for the non-verbal or shy youngster.

While a good art program emphasizes a problem-solving approach, its great advantage is that all the solutions may be different and correct. It can be used to encourage non-conformity because the art results can be unique and individual.

Today we are witnessing an unprecedented interest in and concern for creativity. Much research is underway to reveal the mysteries of this great force. The place of the arts in the general curriculum is to develop the creative aspects of the child's personality in contrast to the subjects which place emphasis on drill, memorization and factual information.

Emphasis has to be put on learning the skills of reading, writing and handling numerical concepts in order that the student can continue to learn and to move ahead in other areas. However, this part of the program stresses conformity because all children must arrive at the same answers.

To balance this we must provide experiences which encourage a variety of answers or non-conformity. Giving children patterns, mimeographed outlines to color, or having them copy, are inhibiting and constricting experiences. The educational impact of such activities is negative and destructive. If a child already feels the least bit insecure in expressing his own ideas, these experiences only reinforce this feeling. Such activities impose rigid stereotypes which destroy the child's confidence in his own concepts.

In one study, a group of children were asked to draw birds. Their drawings were richly conceived with feathers, feet, and beaks drawn in detail. Afterwards the same children were given V-shaped birds to color. A few weeks later, they were asked again to draw birds from imagination. The third time, many of those whose birds once showed detail and imagination now modified their drawings to look more like the V-shaped stereotypes they had absorbed unconsciously.

Recently, after addressing a group of parents, a father related this experience to me. His young son had become interested in drawing turkeys. He drew many different ones, rich in detail and with many variations, and seemed to derive great satisfaction from his efforts. Then, in Sunday School, his teacher gave him a mimeographed outline of a turkey to color in. After he brought this home, he no longer drew turkeys of his own. When his dad questioned him, he replied "I no longer can draw turkeys." The one experience destroyed his confidence in his own ideas.

Sometimes, in our anxiety to get a product, we methodically and unconsciously destroy the greatest power of the child—his imagination. Imagination is a key prerequisite for creativity.

With the tremendous changes occurring so rapidly in our lives, we may need to develop a different kind of person—one who is imaginative and warm and who can respond to people and the world with sensitivity.

Art can help develop such people.

IMAGINATION

Probably the most important faculty that man possesses is his ability to imagine. It was Albert Einstein who said, "Imagination is more important than knowledge." Anatole France felt the same way, "To know is nothing at all, to imagine is everything."

The main purpose of a good art program is to stimulate and nourish this ability to imagine in each child. The following experiences may help do this:

Auditory Stimulus

I. MUSIC (To stimulate visual imagery)
   A. Select a recording with a particular mood.
   B. Do not tell the class its title.
   C. Play it through once with no instructions.
   D. Upon its conclusion, ask if it made them think of anything.
   E. Play it a second time. Now ask them to listen carefully to see if any passages generate a feeling or a visual idea.
   F. At end of record, conduct a more thorough discussion regarding points raised in E.
   G. If teacher feels meaningful responses were achieved, art materials may be passed out and children allowed to illustrate their ideas.
   H. It is more desirable to allow the students some choice in materials or techniques used.
   I. Variations:
      1. Sometimes the emphasis can be on interpreting the rhythm or beat through color and line.
      2. Shades of tissue paper may be used to reproduce tone or mood and a line drawn on top of this to illustrate the rhythm.

II. SOUNDS
   A. Recording or tapes of different sounds (with or without music) are played.
   B. Children can respond to these in the same way as in I above.

Magazine Ads

Save your old magazines or have children bring them to school.

> NOTE: The colored advertisements which appear in so many of our current periodicals such as *Life* or *Look* furnish a wonderful and inexpensive art material. First of all, the colors available are infinitely more varied than the colored construction papers in the schools.
>
> Secondly, many of the colors are rich in texture. Finally, it is easy to change an area or make corrections because all you need to do is paste the new colors over the old ones.
>
> Some of the children could go through these and tear out all of the predominantly red sheets and place them in an envelope so marked. They could do the same with other

colors. Then you would have a selection of colors with which the children could start. If a child needed a special color or texture, he could leaf through the magazines on his own.

When we use these ads, we are interested in using the color in a new way. Discourage, for example, tearing out a tree in a picture and using it as a tree. Instead, if the child plans a tree in his scene, he should make the green foliage out of other green shapes such as parts of mountains, towels, cake frosting and the like. Some interesting mountains were made out of pieces of pancakes.

Skies have been made out of water scenes and vice versa. In this way, we stimulate the child's imaginative and inventive powers.

Thus, the advantages of magazine ads over colored construction paper are:
1. Greater variety of color
2. More possibilities for texture
3. Cost (none)
4. Easy to paste
5. Opportunities to see common objects in new ways; i.e., a pancake becomes a mountain or a tree trunk.
6. Easy to make corrections

The colored advertisements which appear in so many of our periodicals furnish wonderful and inexpensive art material.

 I. ANIMALS
   A. Have each child bring to class 4 or 5 colored magazine ads.
   B. Have him cut and/or tear these into different shapes which can be combined to form an animal—real or imaginary.
   C. These are pasted on a background of colored construction paper.
   D. Black line, details, or texture may be added if necessary.

> NOTE: The shapes made from the ads should be completely different from the subjects in them.

 II. PAPER MOSAICS
   A. Have a child bring in 4 or 5 colored magazine ads.
   B. Give him a 9″ x 12″ black sheet for background.
   C. By tearing the colored areas into mosaic size (thumbnail), have him create a scene or picture entirely different from any of the subjects in the ads.
   D. The torn paper will usually have a white edge which simulates the mortar in a real mosaic so the pieces can touch when pasted.

III. ABSTRACT DESIGNS
   A. Tear at random a number of fairly large shapes from different colored ads.
   B. For contrast a section or two of the classified ads section, or the stock market report from the newspaper may be combined with point A.
   C. Drop or arrange these on a colored background and paste.
   D. Study arrangement. If addition of some smaller shapes would help tie it together or add interest, these may be torn and pasted.
   E. Add details, textures, or lines with black.

Colored Construction Paper

 I. DESIGN, SCENE OR FORM
   A. Tear out freely a large shape or two.
   B. From a different color, tear 3 medium shapes.
   C. From a 3rd color, tear 5 small shapes.
   D. Using your imagination, make the above into a picture, form or design.
   E. Add any shapes needed to complete your idea.
   F. Variations:
      1. Do same with magazine ads.

2. Use colored tissue papers.
3. Combine all three—construction, tissue and ads.

Leaves

I. ANIMALS
   A. Collect different leaves.
   B. Press them for about a week.
   C. Select and arrange them so they form an animal, bird or fish.
   D. When satisfied, mount on colored construction paper with thin line of white glue placed around edge of each leaf.

II. PICTURES OR SCENES
   A. Collect and press a variety of leaves.
   B. Select one or two leaves which will simulate a scene or form.
   C. Mount on paper with white glue.
   D. Complete drawing with crayons, chalk or paint.

Classified Ad Section (Newspaper)

I. CUT OR TEAR AND PASTE
   A. Cut or tear out of a classified ad sheet an animal, building, tree, person, etc.
   B. Paste this on a colored background.

    C. Complete picture or scene with paint, chalk, or crayons.

II. DESIGNS IN CRAYON

    A. Cut a 9″ x 12″ section out of a classified ad sheet. Try to get a page with a predominance of fine print.

    B. Turn sheet so lines dividing columns are horizontal.

    C. With crayons, make a decorative border design along each column.

    D. Use the basic motifs and variations of these—spiral, circle, half-circle, 2 half-circles, wavy line, zigzag line and straight line.

Others

I. INVENTION (Crayon or Chalk)

    A. Invent a new animal.

    B. Place him in an imaginative setting.

    C. Use unusual colors—i.e. pink grass, purple tree trunks, striped or polka dotted bodies.

    D. Correlate with language.

        1. Write a story about your animal.

        2. Describe an adventure he had.

II. START WITH A DOT

    A. Give child 12″ x 18″ dark blue construction paper.

    B. Place a red dot in upper right hand section.

    C. Ask children what ideas are stimulated by this combination.

    D. After discussion, have them complete their ideas with tempera, chalk or colored paper.

III. START WITH A LINE

    A. Give child sheet of paper on which a line has been placed.

    B. Ask child: By adding other lines and colors, what can yours turn into?

    C. Have child complete the picture.

    D. Variations:

        1. Three lines: curved, zigzag, straight.

        2. Outline of a shape.

IV. START WITH A SHAPE

    A. Give each child a sheet of 12″ x 18″ white, manila or light blue background paper.

    B. Give or let him choose an irregular colored scrap (torn or cut).

    C. Have him study this shape and when it stimulates an idea, place it on his background sheet.

    D. Paste shape in place.

    E. Using crayons or paints, complete the picture.

    F. Variations:

        1. Shape may be made out of classified ads, colored magazine advertisements, cloth, or wallpaper.

        2. Picture may be completed with colored papers or collage materials.

COLLAGE

A design or a picture made by pasting or gluing different materials to a flat surface is called a collage. It appeals to the tactile nature of the child because he can work with different textures and materials. Through collage, children can be stimulated to use ordinary materials in new ways.

Collage appeals to the tactile nature of the child.

Materials and Tools

    Boxes (for storing different items)
    Cardboard
    Colored construction paper
    Corrugated paper
    Natural things
        Coffee grounds
        Fine gravel
        Leaves
        Pine needles

Pods
Sand
Seeds
Scraps of cloth
    Burlap
    Patterns
    Solid Colors
    Vegetable sacks
    Velvet
Sandpaper
Small objects
    Beads
    Buttons
    Ice cream sticks
    Toothpicks
Soft things
    Cotton
    Feathers
    Fur
Thin (linear)
    Cord
    Ribbons
    String
    Thread
    Yarn
Transparent
    Cellophane
    Curtain scraps
    Tarlatan
    Theatrical gauze
    Tissue paper
Paste, white glue, or liquid starch
Scissors
Stapler

Motivation

Hold up a piece of cloth with a pattern and ask the children what could it become in a picture. Try to get a variety of responses. Some typical ideas might be:

Through collage, children can be stimulated to use
ordinary materials in new ways.

It could be a dress or a shirt.
It could be a house.
It could be the body of an animal.
It could be a tree.

Do the same with some of the other materials such as a piece of yarn or
rick rack. When you feel most of the children understand, allow them to
start and handle the unsure ones individually.

Procedure

1. Pass out a collection of different materials for each table.
2. Give each child a 9″ x 12″ piece of cardboard, tagboard, or colored
   construction paper, light or dark blue is good.
3. Pass out scissors and paste or glue.
4. Have extra materials on a table or along a counter and work out a way

for children to get these if they need them.
5. Have the children cut and arrange their shapes on the background sheet. When satisfied they may paste them in place.
6. Encourage overlapping or shapes on top of other forms for detail.

Additional Suggestions

1. Colored tissue papers and paint could be combined with collage materials.
2. Have children bring different items for the collage collection. A good way to do this is to have a "button" drive for a few days or a "scrap cloth" drive.
3. Often children's fathers may be the source for interesting scrap materials such as leather, fur, metallic papers or stampings.

10

What Music Can Mean in the Classroom

Dr. Kurt R. Miller

ABOUT THE AUTHOR

Dr. Kurt R. Miller has spent many years bringing teachers and children close to the heart of music. Presently an Associate Professor of Music at the University of Montana, he has served as Supervisor of Fine Arts for the Santa Maria, California School district and Director of Music for the Army Dependents Education Group in Europe. Dr. Miller directed international camps in Switzerland and Denmark and, in 1962, organized the first European summer music camp for American high school students. His text *Help Yourselves to Music*, Wadsworth Co., is used in 30 colleges. He is the music consultant and arranger for the *Exploring Music Series*, Holt, Rinehart and Winston Company.

This is the age of exciting education—teaching which focuses on personal *discovery*, on *creativity*, and on active *participation by the learner*.

In music, this kind of teaching offers unique challenges. Teaching come-alive music-making requires the sharing of one's emotional self plus definite skills not needed elsewhere in the educative process. To "learn" music means music must be actively recreated (discovered). This requires imaginative energy (creativity) and deep personal involvement (participation); music is not accumulated facts or a body of knowledge to be memorized. Music lives for no other reason but that it is an enjoyed, vital, and exciting part of life and is necessary for complete education in our schools.

MEETING INDIVIDUAL NEEDS

Let's begin by "tailoring" our music-making to the youngsters in our own particular class. Let's do things with music so that not only are fresh skills learned and understandings developed, but individual attitudes are also changed along the way.

Begin your successful music program by focusing more on the boys in your room. Sing rousing songs, compliment the boys on their "strong" voices, point up their maleness in every way possible so that it becomes natural for each of your boys to enter into singing—enthusiastically and without feeling his ego is threatened.

Next, arrange songs so that smaller and smaller segments of the class sing portions of a song alone in order to discover and strengthen their own personal abilities.

To illustrate, you might begin by having the class sing:

Marching to Pretoria

English by Josef Marais   South African Folk Song

I'm with you and you're with me, And so we are
We have food, the food is good, And so we will

all to-geth-er, So we are all to-geth-er,
eat to-geth-er, So we will eat to-geth-er,

So we are all to-geth-er. Sing with me, I'll
So we will eat to-geth-er. When we eat, 'twill

sing with you, And so we will sing to-geth-er,
be a treat, And so let us sing to-geth-er,

As we march a-long.— We are

march-ing to Pre-to-ri-a, — Pre-

to-ri-a, — Pre-to-ri-a, — We are march-ing

to Pre-to-ri-a, — Pre-to-ri-a, hur-rah! —

After it has been sung a few times by the class as a whole, divide the singing of the verses:

First verse (girls), second verse (boys), everyone on refrain! At the next singing session *phrases* might also be divided up somewhat like this:

I'm with you and you're with me and so we are all together (Row 1)

So we are all together, so we are all together (Rows 2 and 3)

Sing with me, I'll sing with you and so we will sing together (Row 4)

As we march along (Rows 5 and 6)

Again everyone on the refrain!

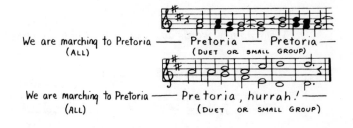

We are marching to Pretoria —— Pretoria —— Pretoria ——
(ALL)   (DUET OR SMALL GROUP)

We are marching to Pretoria —— Pretoria, hurrah! ——
(ALL)   (DUET OR SMALL GROUP)

Later, you might use the *refrain* to challenge the more musical individual children with natural harmonization.

Notice, we think of songs as *tools* to involve small groups and individual children in ways that help them learn more about their personal music capabilities, as well as to develop their own musical skills. We make our singing corrections regarding word pronunciations, pitch intonation, accurate rhythmic singing (plus anything else that will help the music-making sound better), to small groups and to individuals in the class as *they* require it. Learning takes place individually. Becoming aware of each song's natural divisions (phrases, verses and refrain, lines of music, individual words) and using these to involve children separately or in small groups is an important part of music teaching!

NURTURING CREATIVITY

Because a song has "built-in" motions ("This Old Man") or standardized rhythmic accompaniment patterns (the clapping in "Deep in the Heart of Texas") does not necessarily make it a creative music experience.

Children, though, *are* being musically creative as they:

1. Add their own verses to songs:

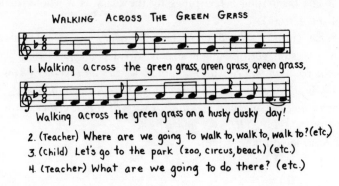

WALKING ACROSS THE GREEN GRASS

1. Walking across the green grass, green grass, green grass,

Walking across the green grass on a husky dusky day!

2. (Teacher) Where are we going to walk to, walk to, walk to? (etc.)
3. (child) Let's go to the park (zoo, circus, beach) (etc.)
4. (Teacher) What are we going to do there? (etc.)

2. Make up new words and many verses to old melodies:

NEW SAN ANTON'
(Tune: OLD GRUMBLER)

We'll sing you a song 'bout a town that we love,

town that we love, town that we love, we'll

sing you a song 'bout a town that we love—San An-ton'.

Interestingly, many United States folksongs require no rhyming of words. These tunes make it possible to rapidly create and sing fresh words (Farmer in the Dell, Ten Little Indians, Jimmy Crack Corn, Mulberry Bush) about *holidays*, such as:

CHRISTMAS BELLS (*Tune:* Are You Sleeping?)
Bells are ringing, bells are ringing,
Hear them ring, hear them ring—
Merry, Merry Christmas, Merry, Merry Christmas
Everyone, everyone.

about *Special Events* in school, such as
DENTAL HEALTH SONG (*Tune:* Mulberry Bush)
This is the way to brush your teeth,
Brush your teeth, brush your teeth.
This is the way to brush your teeth
Early in the morning!

about *celebrations*, such as:

OUR PRINCIPAL CANTATA

In which the class sings a group of folk melodies for their principal using their own words which musically review the highlights of his or her life. (Could this help youngsters understand what it means to "give from the heart"?)

You might find it interesting to have individuals in the class create new and original melodies to standard songs (e.g. "America"). Afterwards, a class discussion pertaining to the strengths and weaknesses of the standard and the new melodies could prove rewarding. To help get the discussion started ask questions about the melodies, such as:

- Does the melody have contrasting parts?
- Does it have unity? (re-occurring patterns)
- Does it have a strong or weak ending?
- Is it interesting?
- What makes it interesting?

3. *Design instrumental accompaniments:*

Many songs gain fresh life by having children add an instrumental accompaniment that reinforces the unique mood and style of the melody and text. For example, try adding a drum beat and interludes of whistling to marching songs ("Marching to Pretoria") or recreate a complete ceremony using flute, tom-tom, rattles and movement to an Indian song.

The gay abandon of our Latin American songs can be expressed better through the addition of an accompaniment using shakers, sticks, scraper and drum. Let the children decide which instruments best reinforce each melody. *Then* ask: "why?".

4. *Interpreting songs through movement:*

Patriotic songs, Christmas carols, hymns and other types of more serious songs easily lend themselves to having their words interpreted in movement. Notice the powerful word-pictures in "America the Beautiful":

AMERICA THE BEAUTIFUL
Oh, beautiful for spacious skies, for amber waves of grain,
For purple mountain majesties, above thy fruited plain.
America, America, God shed his light on thee
And crown thy good with Brotherhood, from sea to shining sea.

To begin, ask the class to "talk to you" through movements using hands and arms (while seated at their desks) as you say each line of "America the Beautiful." After each line, you illustrate (repeat) some of the motions you observed and have the class agree on one for everyone to do. When all lines have thus been "choreographed," have the complete song interpreted in movement by the class as you and a small group sing.

Next, with the class standing, add movements that involve up-and-down (bending, kneeling) as well as patterns of walking (alone or in groups) to the same verse. With a bit of practice your youngsters will be ready to add their own interpretation-in-movement to the opening song, "America the Beautiful" at the next assembly program.

Adding verses, making up new words, developing instrumental accompaniments and moving to songs is creative music learning!

DEVELOPING MUSICALITY

Only by fully experiencing music regularly can we develop an aesthetic sensitivity that becomes a way of life. How do we best help youngsters grow in musical understanding? One way used by successful teachers is to help make them aware of each element that makes the music musical: its movement (rhythm), its sounds (melody) and its expression (style, mood or feelings).

For example, on a song such as the round, "White Coral Bells," we would help the class develop musicality (become aware of musical elements) by asking questions such as:

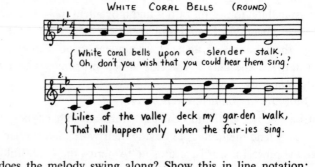

WHITE CORAL BELLS   (ROUND)

{ White coral bells, upon a slender stalk,
{ Oh, don't you wish that you could hear them sing?

{ Lilies of the valley deck my garden walk,
{ That will happen only when the fair-ies sing.

■ How does the melody swing along? Show this in line notation:

$$(— -\ -\ —\ -\ -\ -\ -\ -\ —/— -\ -\ -\ -\ -\ -\ —\ -\ —)$$

■ Direct the meter (4/4) while the class claps the word rhythms. (4/4 meter is directed:)

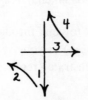

■ Draw the melody pattern on the board.

■ Find the Keytone and Key signature:

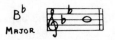

Along with pointing up the musical elements, we would take time to develop sight-singing skills on a regular schedule that progresses from simple to complex such as:

1. Children learn to sing the scale using the numbers 1-2-3-4-5-6-7-1. Then they practice number patterns: 1-3-5-1, 1-5-1, 1-6-4-1, etc.
2. Numbers are sung as written on the staff with the key tone (#1) located on various lines and spaces:

 etc.

3. Scale patterns are sung rhythmically with notes now substituted for numbers:

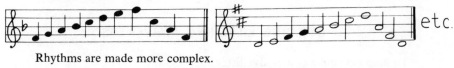 etc.

Rhythms are made more complex.

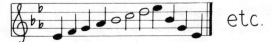 etc.

4. Students are taught how to find the keynote of major scales:

The sharp (#) farthest right is always number *seven* in that scale. Count up one or down seven for the keynote.

No sharps or flats is the key of C major.

The flat (♭) farthest right is always number *four* in that scale. Count up four or down four for the keytone.

5. Children are taught to recognize and understand the meter signature and measures (teach through *hearing* it, then seeing it).

METER is regular, like a heart beat.
METER organizes beats into groups (measures)

$\frac{4}{4}$ METER SIGNATURE—the upper number tells the number of beats in a measure. The lower number tells what kind of note gets one count (quarter note)

6. Children sight-sing simple melodies:

Identify meter signature

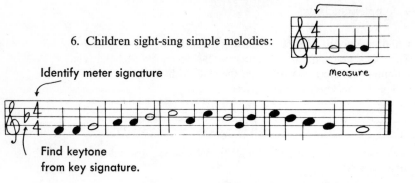

Find keytone
from key signature.

BUILDING LISTENING AWARENESS

To help develop a come-alive listening program:

1. Listen regularly to beautiful music; get the sound "in the air." Children often learn (Heaven-knows-how-much!) for no other reason but that it is expected of them. If your "expectancy-plan" is to listen to beautiful music each day, your children will accept this decision: that beautiful music is part of their environment.

2. Listen more than once to any piece of great music you play . . . it grows on you.

3. Set up a few ground rules for listening such as:

   a. Writing the title and composer of the music to be played on the blackboard.

   b. Telling how long the music will last (½ inch on an LP record equals about 5 minutes playing time). It requires a different kind of attention to listen to 3 minutes of music than to listen to 15 minutes of music.

4. Vary the approach to music-listening through such teaching techniques as:

   a. Comparing selections ("Russian Sailor's Dance" and "Brazilian Dance").

b. Adding rhythm instrument accompaniment occasionally ("Air Gar").
c. Choreographing the music ("Ballet of the Sylphs").
d. Dramatizing the music ("Fairies and Giants").
e. Illustrating the music ("Garden of Live Flowers").
f. Anticipating how the music will sound ("Little Train to Caipera").
g. Reading the story first ("Conversations of Beauty and the Beast."
h. Reading the program notes ("Schubert Symphony No. 5").
i. Beginning with a song ("American Salute" uses as its theme: "When Johnny Comes Marching Home").

All above listed music is from the graded listening program "Adventures in Music"—RCA Victor recordings. A second outstanding classroom record collection is the "Bowmar Listening Series."

Remember, the ability to transfer the language of sound into deep personal experience is a long process. An enthusiastic response to music listening happens only after many listening experiences . . . after you and your pupils have completely accepted a school life that allows a part of each day for being refreshed with beautiful music.

TIE INTO LIFE

Yes, let's build a living environment that refreshes *us* as well as our students. Besides exploring some of the ideas presented above, let's work for more flexibility in our schools (where we are more a family than isolated islands of learning.)

- Let's freely share our talents with other classes by exchange-teaching at times. (Imagine the teacher next door being a drama major. Wouldn't it be logical for her to teach your students how to act in a play?)
- Let's conduct regularly scheduled assembly programs with every class bringing something of interest in the arts to share with the school.
- Let's organize "Enrichment Times" where students can learn in depth about music or some other area of the arts with other youngsters not necessarily from the same class and a teacher who is an expert in that field.
- Let's invite resource people into our schools to demonstrate how the arts and music are a part of their lives and of the community.

- Let's involve district specialists to a far greater degree in our teaching-learning situation and use more audio-visual resources (a ½ hour film on music probably required 500 man-hours of preparation by leading music educators).
- Finally, let's work in music more through *values* which are intrinsic, and self-selective than through *standards* which are imposed, mainly extrinsic and do not recognize individual differences.

As Auntie Mame says, "Life is a banquet, and most poor fools are starving to death." Let's give our youngsters a full banquet of musical experiences.

MUSIC IN YOUR LIFE

Many of us are intrigued with the challenge of living an abundant life. Psychologists believe the answer to making any day or any year rewarding for a person lies in that person's ability to gather vital experiences. The arts and music are one of the finest sources of such experiences known to man. In fact, they exist for that reason only: to fulfill life. Here are a few ideas to help you begin living more abundantly.

- Invite your friends to a "Bring Your Favorite Record" party for an evening of exciting social adventure where guests share their favorite music with each other.
- A phone call to any piano or voice teacher (or to a college music department, if available) would bring you an inexpensive vocal or instrumental solo recital to highlight an evening's entertainment. (Most of us remember years of music study with little or no opportunity to express what we learned.)
- The College (if nearby) will have a schedule of aesthetic events that include concerts by band, orchestra and choral groups, art exhibits in two and three dimensional media, film series, dance and dramatic productions.
- The civic *library* will have, besides books on the arts, recordings of plays and classical music, films for use by service groups, churches, etc., and possibly a lending collection of mounted art reproductions.
- Other civic groups worth exploring include *Civic Theatre* for drama, the *Community Recreation Program* for folk art activities, *Community Concert Programs* for regularly scheduled concerts and *Movies* and *Television* programs in the arts.
- Let's remember that one is never too old to begin private instruction in music. The only requirement here is a desire to learn. School music teachers or a local music store will have recommendations for private teachers. Church and community choirs

are always in need of singers, and joining such a group is really an opportunity to become intimately acquainted with much of the world's great choral literature.

Whether or not one ever becomes a good musician or becomes a good painter, piano player, little theater actor—is almost irrelevant. By simply acquiring even the slightest taste for it, we grow, we change, we develop a keener sense of artistic observation, a deeper appreciation of the aesthetic works of others, and more important, we learn to express ourselves in ever greater capacities. We live more abundantly—and bring much, much more to our students in the classroom.

WHERE-TO-FROM-HERE BIBLIOGRAPHY

To Learn More About Music

Bernstein, Leonard. *The Joy of Music*, Simon and Schuster, 1959.
A lively, highly readable introduction to fine orchestral literature.

Siegmeister, Elie. *Invitation to Music*, Harvey Howe, 1961.
Book and recording illustrating elements that make-up music using excerpts from the world's great music.

To Learn More About Music Teaching:

Andrews, Gladys. *Creative Rhythmic Movement for Children*, Prentice-Hall, 1954.
Still the best comprehensive text on the subject of movement, offers many specific examples. A must.

Krone, B. and K. Miller. *Help Yourselves to Music*, Wadsworth, 1967 (2nd ed.).
Contains numerous approaches for promoting a continuous stream of creative music experiences no matter how meager the teacher's musical background.

Landeck, Beatrice. *Children and Music*, Sloane, 1952.
An informal method of starting music in the home or classroom.

Mathews, Paul W. *You Can Teach Music*, Dutton, 1953.
Down-to-earth advice on presenting music to children although the teacher may have little background in music.

Music for Children's Living, ACEI Bulletin N. 96, 1955.
Forty-eight pages of interesting reading, fine anecdotes and sound advice.

Nye, Robert E. and Bjornar Bergethon. *Basic Music for Classroom Teachers*. Prentice-Hall, 1954.
Ways to bring a creative approach to singing and playing music in the classroom.

Nye, R. and V. Nye. *Music in the Elementary School*. Prentice-Hall, 1964.
> *Surveys all aspects of elementary music teaching by the specialist as well as by the classroom teacher.*

Sheehy, Emma D. *Creating Music with Children*. Holt, 1952.
> *Delightful account of the possibilities offered by music for generating creative growth in children.*

Tiedt, Sidney W. and Iris M. Tiedt. *Elementary Teacher's Complete Ideas Handbook*. Prentice-Hall, 1965.
> *Chapter 9, "Stimulating Musical Interests" offers specific suggestions for encouraging student interest in music.*

Tiedt, Sidney W. and Iris M. Tiedt. *Elementary Teacher's Ideas and Materials Workshop*. Parker Publishing Company, Inc. Monthly Publication.

Free Catalogs Listing Educational Records, Instruments, etc.:

Stanley Bowman Company, Inc., 12 Cleveland St., Valhalla, New York 10595.
> *Contains annotated lists of records, books and filmstrips for the entire music program.*

Children's Music Center, Inc., 5373 West Pico Blvd., Los Angeles, California 90019.
> *Annually prints "The Best Records and Books for the School Curriculum." A catalog listing recommended music materials to enrich various areas of the curriculum.*

Educational Record Sales Company, 157 Chambers St., New York, N.Y. 10017.
> *Distributes "Phonograph and Filmstrips" catalog of musical audio-visual resources in graded categories K–3, 4–6, 7–12, as well as for use in other subject areas such as health, social studies and art.*

Lyons, Incorporated, 223 West Lake St., Chicago, Illinois 60606.
> *Distributes "School Catalog of Musical Needs" that lists rhythm instruments and other audio-visual resources for teaching music.*

Materials for Learning, Incorporated, 1376 Coney Island Ave., Brooklyn, N.Y. 11230.
> *An annually up-dated catalog containing a graded, annotated list of recordings for use in grades K through 6.*

The wealth of new audio-visual materials to help you develop a rewarding music program seems almost limitless. There are recordings to teach your children to harmonize, filmstrip-record combinations that present music theory in a most delightful manner, films that show children developing their creative ideas into movement. Much of this material may already be in your school or school district. Some may be in the county or state resource library. It will pay for you to do a bit of exploring to determine where these materials might be and how you can go about getting them into your classroom.

Then again, if little is available, you may have to request, through your school principal, those helps which seem to have the most immediate worth.

11

New Ways with Old Numbers: Tips for Teaching Mathematics

Dr. Joseph Crescimbeni

ABOUT THE AUTHOR

Joseph Crescimbeni received his Bachelor of Arts degree from Northeastern University in Boston, his Master of Science degree from Fitchburg State College in Massachusetts and his Doctor of Philosophy degree from the University of Connecticut. Presently Professor of Education at Jacksonville University, Jacksonville, Florida, Dr. Crescimbeni also has wide experience as an elementary and secondary school teacher, school administrator, educational consultant, writer and critic.

Dr. Crescimbeni is the author of *Teaching the New Mathematics, Arithmetic Enrichment Activities for Elementary School Children,* and *Guide for Student Teachers.* He has co-authored *Overview of American Education* and *Guiding the Gifted Child.* He has written many articles for such journals as *Education, The Saturday Review, The NEA Journal, Kappa Delta Pi, Child and Family* and *The Connecticut Teacher.*

The term "new mathematics" is being used and often misused by parents, children and teachers. It becomes necessary, therefore, for an understanding of a simplified definition of this term in order that teachers, parents and children will become fairly comfortable with it. Basically, new mathematics means a new emphasis on a subject field, taught by modern methods based on a new psychology of learning and executed with modern tools. But it also means something new in *content* as well as *approach*. The purpose is to replace numb learning of rote computation with a confident understanding of the structure and relationship of numbers. This means the why of the drills. Rules and formulas are still vital tools, but "new math" aims to go back to the source of the rules to show why they are valid, rather than blindly prescribing them.

Beginning with elementary arithmetic, new mathematics places an emphasis on concepts. By shifting emphasis from the mechanical to the creative, more teachers see that children will be better able to cope with new developments requiring mathematical competencies in this age of the atom and space exploration.

Research has shown that much of the mathematics traditionally taught at the junior high and senior high school levels could be absorbed by children in the elementary grades, if *presented properly* and at the conceptual phase of *their understanding*. As a result, instruction in many topics now begins in the primary grades and a *developmental* system of mathematics instruction has been the result. This type of teaching has nurtured a high degree of interest from elementary pupils. It has fostered a great deal of creative expression in finding solutions to old mathematical problems. It has also brought about a renaissance in teaching this area. But most of all, it has made arithmetic instruction challenging and fun to pupils!

Characteristics of the "new mathematics approach" include the following elements:

1. Explanations are given of the *why* as well as the *how*. Everything the child does in number manipulation has a reason. He understands these reasons.
2. A great deal of deductive reasoning and proof is utilized. Basic laws of logic are applied. A child knows the reasons behind an operation and this assists him in discovering the mathematical process in the relationships of numbers.
3. Structure of mathematics is emphasized. Mathematics is an organized body of knowledge. As such, basic laws of operation apply to its application.
4. Teaching is done in the form of "heuristic learning." This is commonly called the discovery method. The child uses questions and illustrative examples to make and test ideas of his own. The best learning occurs when he "sees" the concept on his own. This form of insight allows the pupil to retain his discoveries for longer periods of time and makes him realize his mathematical work is worth something.
5. Emphasis is placed on precise use of language. Definitions are stated carefully and applied at all times. The ability to read

mathematics problems intensively for meaning is essential to success.

6. New mathematics is built on unifying ideas that are essential for the understanding of more advanced mathematics. This allows for less unlearning and relearning as the child reaches higher levels of learning in this subject.

The *first tip* in teaching is then to tell children why they are learning this way. Once the mystery of the why is presented, children attack their mathematics problems with vigor as well as understanding. Children must know why arithmetic is important in the elementary curriculum. They must understand the relative roles of meaning and drill. They must realize and accept the social usage of mathematics in their adult lives.

The *second tip* in teaching is for teachers to *personalize* this instruction with their children. No longer can we use basal arithmetic texts for *all* children in the class. We know that children are different in size, learning ability and in their interests of pursuits. Therefore, teaching new mathematics must be predicated upon interest, aptitude, readiness of learning and understanding of individual children. Although we accept the principle of individual differences, we only give lip service to it in the classroom.

The *third tip* for teachers is that the application of mathematical understandings can be done in challenging and intriguing ways. Although the market is filled with devices and instructional aids for teaching elementary arithmetic, teachers should be creative and use their own methods and their own classroom-made materials for implementing these concepts. Children, when given the opportunity, are very creative and often think of instructional aids that will help them in their mathematical understandings. Consequently, teachers must set a stage for learning and they must be ready to see the creative child and use his talents in applying mathematical understandings to him as well as to other members of the class.

Being creative and teaching with challenge then places a tremendous responsibility on the teacher. The teacher must be alert and perceptive if she is going to individualize her arithmetic instruction to her pupils. As we have grouping in reading instruction, we should have *grouping by ability* in mathematical instruction. Teachers must learn to use different instructional materials for different levels of instruction. They must employ different ways of performing operations with children. Teachers must use different ways to solve verbal problems. And they must provide conditions where children discover mathematical principles.

To implement these conditions in the classroom teaching atmosphere, the author is an exponent of arithmetic enrichment aids. The more diverse the aids, the better the quality of understanding. The more individualized the aids to the mathematical learning principle, the better the child will respond to this type of teaching. Teaching arithmetic then becomes prescriptive in nature. We diagnose the children's deficiencies and weaknesses and prescribe a corrective learning exercise for them. This type of *prescriptive teaching* is based not only on grouping by ability but also by grouping of *mathematical deficiencies*. There is a difference, and the perceptive and sensitive classroom teacher recognizes it immediately. When a teacher is conducting a mathematical lesson with ten or fifteen different learning principles she is then adhering to this type of prescriptive teaching.

Lastly, teachers must differentiate the *type* of mathematical teaching now being done in the classroom. It must be updated and of interest. It must be socially applicable. It must be practical and it must be initially interesting and challenging. Then children are ready to learn and eager to learn. They do not manifest "mental blocks" toward learning, and these psychological blocks were much in evidence in the American classrooms before this decade.

The rest of this chapter will deal with tips for teaching in particular situations. There is not enough room in this chapter to make it all-inclusive but the ideas presented here may become a springboard for teachers to use their initiative and their creativeness for making arithmetic instruction more than a daily chore. These ideas may also help the teacher to allow children to become creative in their understanding and approach to mathematical learnings and to contribute *their* ideas for a deeper and more comprehensive appreciation.

Tips on Teaching Terms

The history of numbers is filled with facts and folklore about terms and methods of measurement, of weight, of area, of volume, etc. Children should be exposed to the origin of these terms and then make comparative analysis of their application in the classroom. For instance:

Girth —was originally the length of a string around the waist of an individual.

Cubit —was an Egyptian term that became the distance from the elbow to the tip of the middle finger. (Some people still use this form of estimation.)

Span —The distance of the outspread hand from the thumb to the tip of the little finger. (Can you guess how often we use this form of measurement today? and in what situations?)

Fathom—With both hands outstretched, the fathom was the distance between the finger tips.

Foot —the length of a particular man's foot. (Ask the children why this is impractical in accurate measurement.)

Step —the length of one particular man's step.

Pace —the equivalent of two steps.

Inch —the distance equal to 1/12 of a man's foot. Edward II of England decreed it should be the width of three barley corns taken from the middle ear of corn. (Ask the children to do this project in the classroom. Are some barley corns different in size?)

Rod —Originated in Germany. It was established by stopping 16 men, some tall and some short as they exited from a Sunday morning church service. As they stepped out and they walked directly behind the other, the length of the 16 men was decreed to be the lawful measure to survey the land.

- Have the children discover the fallacy of these measurements. As another project, have them establish these forms of measurement according to their estimation and then objectify by using a ruler and a yardstick. Is there a difference in the recorded measurements? How much of a difference? Why is accuracy in measurement important? Can you think of some misgivings if inaccuracy in measurement is allowed?

Tips on Teaching Number Sentences

Number sentences express ideas in the same way that word sentences express ideas. Children must realize that each part of a number sentence has a specific meaning. And also, it has a definition in the terms of sentence structure. Illustrate by this example:

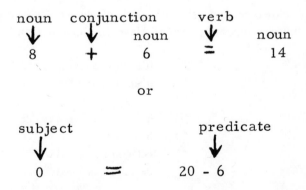

- Have the children form number sentences and label each part. Teach them open sentence, true sentence statement, false sentence statement, equivalent and non-equivalent sentence statements. Have them make a chart identifying each of these number sentences. Have them write the equivalent English sentence for each of the number sentences they have selected.

Tips on Teaching a Circle

A circle is a closed curve. Parts of circles, composed of lines or line segments, also have specific names. Have the child look at the following diagram and then learn the parts. Do they associate them in everyday patterns in the classroom? At home?

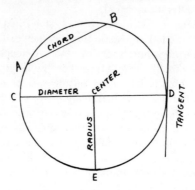

- Ask the class what familiar object with a moving part continually changes its radius and diameter positions?   (*Answer*: a clock)
- Have the class draw different size circles. Compare the line parts of the circles. Does it make a difference what length the radius is, or the chord is, or the tangent is in order to be called such?

Tips on Teaching Polygons

A simple closed curve consisting entirely of segments is a polygon. There are many different types of polygons. Have the children identify each of the following:

△	triangle	3 sides
⬠	quadrilateral	4 sides
⬠	pentagon	5 sides
⬡	hexagon	6 sides
◯	heptagon	7 sides
◯	octagon	8 sides
◯	decagon	10 sides

- Have them find pictures representing these polygons. Take a tour of the school and see how many polygons you can identify. How are they used in construction? In the manufacture of specific items? Can they name some.
- Have them cut these figures out of oak-tag. Also, they can make these figures with colored string.

Some Tips in Teaching Sets

Set teaching has become common in the primary grades. Children learn that they have a set of parents, sets of toys, sets of clothing, sets of arms, legs, etc. At the primary level we can show them what sets look like:

a, b, c, f, z .... a set of letters

3, 4, 5, 6, 9 .... a set of numbers

.... a set of shapes

.... a set of toys

EQUIVALENT SETS

Equivalent sets are sets that can be paired with one another. Look at the items in this set. Have the children draw lines to pair them off.

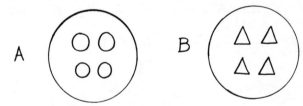

NON-EQUIVALENT SETS

How does this set differ from the one above?

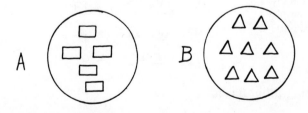

Tips on Teaching Bases

A base system is a method of value measurement. We assign a specific representation for something that gives us a specific value of that picture. Picture symbols are repeated to name a desired quantity or number. Position of the symbol is important in reading meaning. Our base system is called the *decimal system* because of the ten symbols used in it:

Namely: 1, 2, 3, 4, 5, 6, 7, 8, 9, 0.

Children easily learn other base systems and one good exercise is to have them devise their own base system based on their own symbols. They can then express numeration and solve problems. For example:

BASE TEN	CHILD'S DEVISED SYSTEM
1.	◯
2.	△
3.	▢
4.	⊙
5.	☌
6.	▽
7.	—
8.	=
9.	▯
0.	⊓

- After devising their system, have them formulate some number problems and then solve the problems based on their own base system: (Note–each child can use a different picture value representation)

  Example 1: $⊙ - △ + = + ◯ = 11$

  Example 2: $▯ - ⊙ + ☌ = 10$

  Example 3: $◯ + △ + ▢ + — = 13$

- Now, make it more difficult by using other more complex operations:

  Example 1: $▽ × △ + ◯ = 13$

  Example 2: $= ÷ ⊙ × △ = 4$

  Example 3: $▢ × ▢ × ◯ = 9$

Tips on Teaching Other Bases

A base means a grouping of symbols on a *specified value*. An easy way to have children understand this operation is to draw a series of picture symbols and then name what base they would like to be in. Circling the symbols according to the base grouping then becomes illustrative of the quantity and value for each grouping. Look at these examples:

PICTURE	BASE	DECIMAL EQUIVALENT
	3	$(3 + 1) = 4$
	4	$(4 + 3) = 7$
	5	$(15 + 1) = 16$
	6	$(6 + 4) = 10$
	7	$(7 + 3) = 10$
	8	$(8 + 1) = 9$
	9	$(18 + 2) = 20$

- Have the children place meaningless symbols in groups and then assign a base numeration. Then have them convert the symbols into the base value and make it equivalent to our decimal system.
- As an additional exercise, have symbols in base ten and have the children regroup them into several different bases of their own choice.

This interchange of base activity develops understanding and recognition of value to symbol relationship. It enforces their comprehension of the base system and allows them to easily convert any number, into any base system with ease and accuracy.

Tips on Teaching Triangles

There are many different types of triangles. Teach children the types that they may see around the school or the home. This upper grade activity can be supplied with social usage.

Equilateral—three equal sides
Isosceles—two equal sides
Scalene—no equal sides

Right angle triangles

Right triangle—one right angle
Obtuse angle triangle—one obtuse angle
Acute angle triangles—all angles acute

Geometric Riddle Quiz

Have your young children ask themselves these riddles. After they give you the answer, have them draw the figure that they represent with their answer:

	Answer
I have three sides. What am I?	triangle
I have no sides. What am I?	circle or ball
I have four sides the same length and four equal angles. What am I?	a square
I am round but flat on one end, and pointed on the other end. What am I?	a cone

Teaching Tips for Reasoning

Reasoning is an important phase in new mathematics. Children must be given numerous situations where they will use their powers of reasoning for estimation. Throughout the entire arithmetic curriculum such opportunities arise. Here are some illustrations with decimal reasoning: Give the children the statement and have them circle their reasoned response.

1. If you multiply 5.60 by .8 the product will be MORE or LESS than 5.60.   (Less)
2. If you multiply .49 by 1.25 the product will be MORE or LESS than .49.   (More)
3. If you multiply .005 by .05 the product will be MORE or LESS than .005.   (Less)

4. If you multiply .55 by 32 the product will be MORE or LESS than .55.   (More)

- Use this same form of reasoning with examples in fractions, mixed numbers, and like and unlike fractions. Estimation can be a valuable reasoning concept that will prove useful in higher forms of mathematical instruction.

Teaching Tips for Drill Activity

Arithmetic drill is an important part of the daily program. If drill is used properly and with purposeful direction, its carryover value is valuable to children. Consider drill activity with careful planning:

1. Drill should be short and intensive.
2. Drill should be specific. Place your emphasis on one specific concept rather than many concepts.
3. Compare drill lessons with previous drill activities in order to compare growth.
4. Drill should provide accuracy and speed in computation.
5. Never consider drill as busy work. This defeats your purposeful planning for this type of reinforcement.
6. Have the children correct drill activities. Discovering their own mistakes is an excellent learning factor and is more retentive.

General Teaching Tips

Every teacher needs to explore the aptitude and interests of each pupil. Predicated upon these findings she needs to arrange a series of exercises and activities geared to these discovered needs. Listed below are some general teaching tips and some activities worthy of pursuit. Such activities and teaching tips help to make the daily arithmetic lesson a motivating challenge which will direct children to further mathematical experiences.

1. Always see that every child experiences *some success* in his daily work. You can individualize your activities to insure success and understanding. Success breeds interest and continuing performance.
2. Avoid *useless repetition* of learning when it is not needed. Do not over-assign practice examples as busy work or as punishment activity.
3. *Stress problem solving* and problem comprehension. Reading and interpreting mathematical problems correctly is an important aspect of the program.
4. *Providing number stories* as an enrichment activity. Stories dealing with number problems are abundant and should be part of each child's experience.

5. Allow the children to *make a glossary of math terms* on 3" x 5" cards or oak-tag. The child who has the fingertip knowledge of math term definitions can use this resource to help him solve problems.

6. Try to teach arithmetic activities in *small groups*. This provides for individual differences and helps correct existing deficiencies.

7. *Do not rely* totally on basal texts in arithmetic. Construct home-made devices and have the children formulate real problems for deeper understanding. Social application of arithmetic activity is of vital use.

8. *Motivate* your teaching lessons with visual material. The more extensive the use of aids the better and higher the pupil interest.

9. Give frequent quizzes to *determine learning weaknesses* rather than to determine achievement. We are interested in overcoming what we don't know rather than testing what we do know.

10. *Carefully plan your lessons* for each small group. Repetition of one activity of a particular group to another group soon discourages the child. Each child wants to have "special attention" through the preparation of special work.

11. *Use the tape recorder* for drill activities. Have the child use the tape recorder upon which you have prepared math problems in the four operations in an increasing order of difficulty. Have the children mentally compute your question and then write their answers.

12. *Insist upon good work habits.* Do not allow children to do careless work, with no visible computation at the initial stages of new work presented. Good work habits are a must for every child.

13. *Provide self-checking lessons.* In the form of a ditto sheet or workbook activity, self-checking builds confidence and competence in the pupil to examine and evaluate his own work.

14. Use arithmetic tests *as a diagnostic measure.* Always have the child see what examples he has misunderstood and executed improperly. Try to have him discover his mistakes. If he fails in this attempt, then instruct him as to the proper identified procedure.

15. *Make arithmetic fun.* Like all other areas of the elementary curriculum, good mind set is important. Make learning fun! Through an emphasis on the child's self-concept for success, learning will take on a new dimension.

12

The Cuisenaire Method as an Approach to Modern Math

Sister Ann Boland, S.U.S.C.

ABOUT THE AUTHOR

Sister Ann Boland, S.U.S.C., received her Bachelor of Science degree from Catholic Teacher's College in Providence, Rhode Island. For the past five years she has been director of the Holy Union Pre-School in Fall River, Massachusetts.

Introducing young children to an understanding of abstract numbers has always been a challenge to the teachers of beginning learners. In our Pre-School, I have found the *M. Cuisenaire Method* of arithmetic computation to be exceedingly valuable and feel it would be so throughout the elementary school grades.

I was first introduced to this method by Sister Mary Richard Aurich, who piloted a program of experimentation in Saint Mary's Elementary School in Taunton, Mass., with fantastically successful results.*

A child uses logic and reasoning in the manipulation of concrete objects, but does not do so with mere verbal expression. The abstract ideas of mathematics can be easily learned by the youngest students through concrete manipulative experiences. The most helpful mathematical tools of this nature are the Cuisenaire Colored Rods. These rods hold a magnetic appeal for younger, as well as for older children. They can be used effectively in non-graded situations where each child discovers his own level and progresses at his own rate of learning.

Cuisenaire rods are stained pieces of wood from one to ten centimeters

---

*A full treatment of the method is presented in Sister's dissertation entitled, *A Comparative Study to Determine the Effectiveness of the Cuisenaire Method of Arithmetic Instruction with Children at the First Grade Level* submitted at Catholic University of America in partial fulfillment of the requirements for the Degree of Master of Arts.

in length. Three rods have the basic pigment red; three have blue; two, yellow; one is unstained, and one is black. The unstained rod is one centimeter long. All the other rods' lengths are multiples of this, in an ascending scale:

White	— 1 centimeter
Red	— 2 centimeters
Light Green	— 3 centimeters
Purple	— 4 centimeters
Yellow	— 5 centimeters
Dark Green	— 6 centimeters
Black	— 7 centimeters
Brown	— 8 centimeters
Blue	— 9 centimeters
Orange	—10 centimeters

When the unstained rod is made to represent the unit one, the rods in the red pigment group represent 2, 4, 8; those in the blue represent 3, 6, 9; those in the yellow 5, 10; the black rod is 7 times the unstained rod.

This method of using color in mathematics was discovered by M. Georges Cuisenaire, a retired director of education for Thurin, the Belgian Province of Hainaut. As a well known progressive primary teacher he observed the difficulties encountered by children engaged in mathematical studies and devised this imaginative approach which makes the teaching of arithmetic concepts a delight.

Free Play Period

I am accustomed, for the first few weeks of class, to place the rods on a low table where I permit and encourage complete freedom to explore, to measure, to compare, to build, to tear down and to rebuild.

Michael puts the finishing touches on his tower during "free play" period.

In this way the rods become a favorite activity during free choice periods. They soon become an important asset in establishing meaningful communication among the children.

During these early days, colors are learned or reviewed as the need may be. A mathematical vocabulary is established; concepts of space and relationship such as the following are explored: *over, beside; big, bigger, biggest; tall, taller, tallest; small, short; first, second, third, etc.*

If the teacher listens to the children during this Free Play Period, she may hear comments such as "Orange rods make the best foundation; they're the biggest." "See, five red rods make one orange."

At this time no formal instruction is given. The teacher observes, encourages, and discusses the discoveries made by the children. Questions can be posed to help the less creative youngster discover, such as, "Which rod is the tallest?" "the shortest," etc. In this way, a great love of rod work is established in very little time.

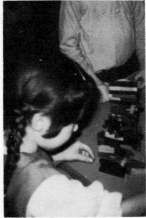

The children work together with their colored sticks—building, measuring, etc.

Oral Work

When the fondness for working with the rods is developed, a formal program can begin. At this time, oral work is most important. The children verbalize their findings to the teacher. The older children help younger students by listening as they speak of their discoveries.

Susan listens as Brian calls his "trains."

Written Work

Eager to "show and tell" their new discoveries at home, the children are ready now for some paper work. This consists of matching and measuring, like the following samples:

Worksheet   A

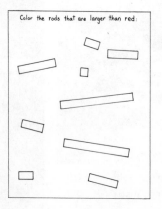

Color the rods that are larger than red:

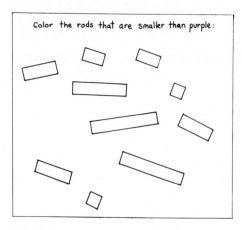

Color the rods that are smaller than purple:

Worksheet   B

Draw a circle around pairs of rods:
Color the larger one the correct color.

Worksheet   C

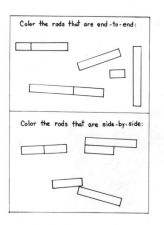

Color the rods that are end-to-end:

Color the rods that are side-by-side:

Worksheet   D

Worksheet   E

Martha is busy matching the rods and coloring one of the first exercise papers.

Addition

Soon the children begin to seek for new information. Addition is started with the introduction of "trains." A train is made by placing the rods end to end. See illustration below.

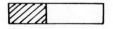

The children feel this train while speaking of it, for example, "I have a red plus a green train" or "A red plus a green train is the same size as one yellow rod."

The children continue their coloring and matching exercises until they search out a quicker way of recording their findings. When the teacher perceives this need for speed, she presents the letter names of the rods.

w — white		d — dark green	
r — red		k — black	
g — light green		n — brown	
p — purple		e — blue	
y — yellow		o — orange	

Young children are not acquainted with the spelling of the color words, I therefore arrange large construction paper representations of the rods on a bulletin board with the letter names attached. This year we had Winnie the Pooh ascending a large red staircase.

Trains can now be recorded.

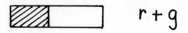

r + g

Robert is recording his "train."

The plus sign $(+)$ is introduced as a directional sign. As the traffic light is a tool to a road driver, so the plus sign is to the mathematician. Plus $(+)$ acts as a link between the cars, permitting the youngsters to experiment with both equal and equivalent statements.

EQUAL:

$$p + r = p + r$$

EQUIVALENT:

$$d = g + g$$
$$d = r + p$$
$$g + g = r + p$$
$$r + p = g + g$$
$$r + p = d$$
$$g + g = d$$

Equals $(=)$ are shown as a scale. The rods are so well proportioned that their actual weight can be balanced. *For example*: two red rods balance with a purple rod; or one unstained rod and a light green. This knowledge helps the child visualize that one number has many names. Many facts can be discovered and illustrated in equations by the formation of one simple train.

ONE TRAIN

$$d = r + r + r$$
$$d = 2r + r$$
$$d = 3r$$
$$3r = d$$
$$r + r + r = d$$
$$d - 2r = r$$
$$d - r = 2r$$
$$\tfrac{1}{3} \times d = r$$
$$\tfrac{2}{3} \times d = 2r = p$$
$$\tfrac{3}{3} \times d = 3r = d$$
$$d \div r = 3$$

The children are inductively learning the commutative and associative properties of Addition, for example:

COMMUTATIVE:

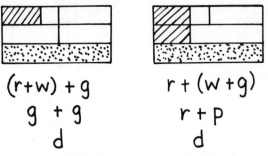

COMMUTATIVE:

$$y + w = w + y$$

ASSOCIATIVE:

ASSOCIATIVE:

$$(r+w) + g$$
$$g + g$$
$$d$$

$$r + (w + g)$$
$$r + p$$
$$d$$

The concept of subtraction is presented simultaneously with addition. Trains lead naturally to big cities with apartment houses. Standing the rods on their ends and placing them *side by side* with other rods, we discover the differences in height. Below is an illustration, pointing out the method of arranging and recording the subtraction equations.

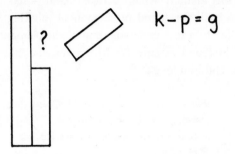

By this time, the numerals have become a definite part of the child's spoken vocabulary, "Please hand me two red rods, five yellows," etc. Such requests come quite naturally at this point. It is an easy step, now, to introduce them to the numerical symbols by means of matching games, and handwriting exercises.

I use the rods as well as other types of Primary Grade materials to discuss sets of objects and to develop the concept of number and numeral. *For example*: the children count blocks, sticks and similar things. They work with the flannel boards, the abacus, bead frames and other traditional materials. This procedure is necessary since most of these children transfer to traditional classrooms. It will be helpful, therefore, for them to have experienced various methods. In a few weeks the rods are seen in relation to mathematical problems. Multiplication, division, fractions, etc. are discovered. We begin to associate numerals with the rods. In a very short time, all the letter work they accomplished is transferred into numerical notation.

Games

To make arithmetic more than paper work, to keep it alive and in the realm of reality, I have found the game "Shopping" most profitable. The children make small pocketbooks in which to carry their money, in this case, the rods. Four or five stores are set up successively, The Ribbon Shop, where any type of tape, lace, or ribbon is sold by the inch—one inch for one cent. The inches are marked off on the counter of the play store forming a large version of the rod staircase.

A Lemonade Stand is next. Here we use all sorts of measures,—one cent for one ounce. Water dyed with food coloring is stored in pint, quart, and gallon containers. Candy and Toy stores may be added. Advanced students would find a Grocery Store more of a challenge. All the children take turns buying and selling, recording their own bills. All computation of the bills is done at the rod table.

By means of this method which involves hand, mind and eye in simultaneous action, a basis for sound mathematical thinking is developed, and the child can be led to a real understanding of the elementary mathematical relationships by firsthand experience. Moreover, the creative play element is strong, and the children love it.

For the current catalog of Cuisenaire materials and books, write to:
Cuisenaire Company of America, Inc.
9 Elm Avenue
Mt. Vernon, New York 10550

Books:

Brideoake Co. *Arithmetic in Action.* London: University of London Press, 1939.

Gattegno Co. *Mathematics with Numbers in Color.* New York: Cuisenaire Company of America, Inc., 1938.

Judith, Sister Mary and Anthony, Sister Marie. *Discovering Truth in Numbers.* New York: Cuisenaire Company of America, Inc. 1963.

Stern and Gould. *Structural Arithmetic.* Boston: Houghton Mifflin Company, 1965.

Suppes, Patrick. *Sets and Numbers.* L. W. Singer Company, Inc., 1965.

Thoburn, Tina and McGraith, Lucille. *Greater Cleveland Mathematics Program.* Chicago: Science Research Associates Inc., 1962.

Periodicals:

Cuisenaire Reports
Cuisenaire Company of America, Inc.
9 Elm Avenue, Mount Vernon, N.Y. 10550

Films:

Mathematics at Your Fingertips
Nation Film Board of Canada
Dept. C, 680 Fifth Avenue
New York 10019
Subtraction with the Cuisenaire Rods
Martin Moyer Productions
900 Federal Avenue
Seattle 2, Washington

13

Science: A Highpoint of the Day

Robert J. Michalek

ABOUT THE AUTHOR

Robert J. Michalek received the Bachelor of Science Education degree from Northern Illinois University and the Master of Education degree from Harvard University. He has completed additional work at the University of Illinois on Teaching the gifted. Mr. Michalek spent 13 years in the classroom and was head of both the science and mathematics departments at Hinsdale Junior High School. Since 1965 he has been principal of the Elm Elementary School in Hinsdale. He wrote the Teacher's Manual for the *7th Grade Understanding Arithmetic* published by Laidlaw Brothers. Mr. Michalek has directed the summer reading program for second and third graders in the Hinsdale school district. Since 1966 he has conducted a series of workshops for elementary teachers on teaching gifted and creative students. He is a science consultant for the Hinsdale schools.

Science offers the elementary teacher a wonderful opportunity for dynamic teaching in the elementary school. Many teachers faced with problems of motivation ask themselves, "What can I do?" One answer is to brainstorm your way to solutions. The game of brainstorming follows five rules.

1. *No evaluation of any kind is allowed in a thinking-up session.*
   If you judge and evaluate as ideas are thought up, the person whose idea is questioned will be more concerned with defending

the idea than he will be in thinking up new and better ones. Evaluation must be ruled out.

2. *All are encouraged to think of ideas which are as wild as possible.* It is easier to tame down than to think up. Actually, if wild ideas are not forthcoming, internal evaluation is probably going on in the minds of the individual participants. They are thinking twice before they spout an idea for fear that they may come up with a silly one, and therefore look foolish.

3. *Quantity of ideas is encouraged.* Quantity eventually breeds quality, but more important, quantity also helps to rule out evaluation.

4. *Everyone is encouraged to build upon or modify the ideas of others.* Combinations or modifications of previously suggested ideas often lead to new ideas superior to those that sparked them.

5. *Jot down your ideas!* Yes, jot them down! Don't throw out what at first may seem ridiculous for frequently this turns out—with slight alterations—to be your best bet.

Brainstorming resulted in many of the ideas which fill this chapter. Use them as they are—or use them as springboards for your own brainstorming sessions and see what evolves for your classroom!

■ *Combine the activity of slide making with growing mold on bread.* (Don't underestimate your pupil's ability. This has been done with fourth graders.) Divide the class into small groups and each group does the following:

You will need:
    a microscope slide
    a microscope slide cover glass
    some paper towels
    forceps
    bottle of balsam or dammar
    small label or gummed paper cut to use as a slide label.

1. Wash slide with water, dry with towel.
2. Remove lint with lens paper or a clean paper towel. Lay the clean slide on a clean paper towel.
3. Place a drop of balsam on the middle of the slide.
4. Into this balsam (sometimes called dammar), with forceps, carefully place some of the mold from moldy bread.
5. Add a drop or two more of dammar over this.
6. Using forceps, carefully lower a clean cover glass so one edge touches the dammar and then let it go so the whole glass covers the dammar. If the cover glass is lowered in place in this manner air bubbles will not be trapped under the cover slip. Press cover slip gently but firmly with pencil tip. DO NOT TOUCH ANY OF THE BALSAM.
7. Set slide on a towel with your name on it and set this in a cabinet to dry. (This will take about one or two weeks or longer.)

8. After drying, excess dammar is scraped off with a sharp knife, care being taken that the cover glass is not moved. Do not get knife near the cover glass. Only scrape the dry dammar to make the slide neat.

9. Label the slide.

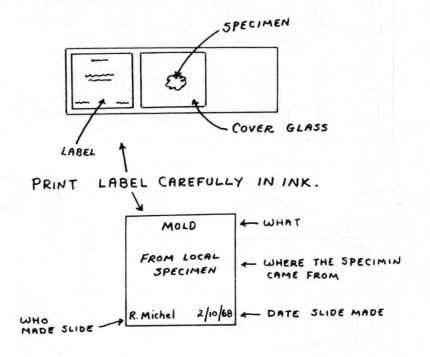

■ Many things are brought to the teacher's desk from pupils and the post office! When the mail arrives, even advertising brochures, ask yourself, "What can I do with this? How can I relate it to science?" *Make a classroom Science Corner with Things of Science—* or display them in the school's showcases.

Once you figure out a display, make a sketch of it and keep the materials in a large expandable envelope to be used another year. For instance,

1. Read the pamphlet (brochure, bulletin, article, etc.) and/or look at the material.
2. Decide what you can use.
3. Make a display sketch.
4. Use a primary typewriter and write out what you think is interesting. (This may not be the most important part; it can be left for the student to figure out.)
5. Give the display a catchy title.
6. If possible, let students do something within the display.

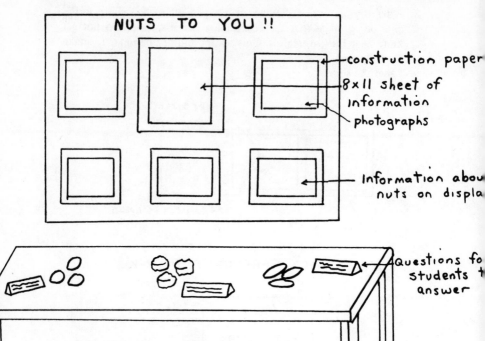

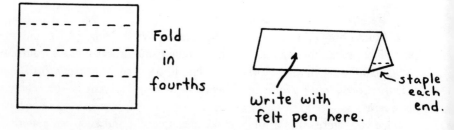

Display Table

7. On your table fold a sheet of construction paper to form a stand-up triangle.

Fold in fourths

write with felt pen here.

staple each end.

- On these triangles write questions or tell things students can do. Examples:

  CAN YOU TELL HOW MANY POUNDS OF NUTS THE AVERAGE PERSON EATS IN A YEAR?

  HOW CAN YOU TELL NUTS HAVE OIL?

  WHEN IS A NUT NOT A NUT?

- You may even have an answer box and have a contest for "Scientist of the Month."

■ If you are a Science Consultant, have you ever tried *publishing your own science newspaper* for teachers in your district? The articles you put in can be of almost endless variety:

1. Recent developments in science.
2. News items of interest.
3. Suggested activities.
4. Alternate ways of conducting experiments.
5. Book reviews.
6. New science materials.

Vol. I- No. 2   25 November 1967

HINSDALE

SCIENCE EYE

LEAVES
Got some beautiful leaves you wish you could save and preserve their colors? Well, you can if you wipe them well on both sides with a piece of cotton rag that has been moistened with glycerine (the kind that you buy in the drug store). Wipe both sides of the leaf while it is resting on wax paper. When dry, it can be pressed and mounted on paper. Leaves that have been treated this way have been known to hold until the following year.

BODY CELLS
Sixth grade teachers, if you are studying the human body, can have students see their own body cells by letting them gently scrape the inside of their cheeks with a flat toothpick and make a smear on a microscope slide. Under the microscope the cells will look like this:

CELL ⬭ ⬭ ⬭ NUCLEUS
CELL MEMBRANE

These cells are typical Squamous Epithelial cells. Ahem!!!

FREE POSTERS
The Ford Motor Company, Detroit, has a series of free charts available to teachers. A timely chart included is: "How an Automobile is Tested". Write for these 16x22 charts that are folded and punched for 3-ring binders. Also included are three charts 24x22 showing the evolution of the Ford, Lincoln, and Mercury.

NEW BOOK
Each building should now have the book, Elementary Teacher's Class-room Science Demonstrations and Activities by Hennessy. Use it as an enrichment to the text.

HEAT ENERGY
Stretch a rubber band while holding it close to your lips. Immediately after stretching it, hold it to your lower lip. It will feel quite warm. This is due to excitation of the molecules or in-creasing their kinetic energy which is what heat is-- the kinetic energy of the molecules.

PLANT CELLS FOR FIFTH GRADE ST STUDY
To see plant cells under the microscope, use an onion. Remove the dry skin from an onion and then carefully remove a thin skin from one of the layers of the onion and place a piece of this in the center of a glass slide. Place a drop of weak iodine solution (called Lugol's solution) on the specimen and cover with a glass microscope cover clip. Nice oblong cells will be seen with little dark round nuclei.

COMIC BOOKS FOR 6TH GRADE
General Electric has comic-format booklets which they will provide at no cost. If you are a 6th grade teacher and desire quantities of these, fill in the coupon below and return it by Dec-ember 4. As soon as they arrive, they will be distributed to you.
Please send me the following:
____ copies of INSIDE THE ATOM, an account of atomic structure and atomic energy (fission and fusion).
____ copies of OUR PLACE IN SPACE, the nature of a missile and types of missiles and space vehicles.
____ ADVENTURES IN JET POWER. the development of jet flight and the principle involved.
____ ADVENTURES IN ELECTRONICS what electronics is, applications to home industry and military.
Name_____
School_____

■ For an end-of-the-year science project *have each child bring a toy and write a paper about how it works.* Be sure they use the scientific principle involved. If you have time, let them exchange toys and papers and see if others understand or can find flaws or omissions in the explanations.

■ Have you ever done anything with *science fiction stories*? The best are those which incorporate facts. Space science fiction stories lend themselves well to this activity:

1. Have pupils select one planet they would like to visit.
2. Begin with their landing on the planet.
3. Have each one research facts on the planet (on satellite, comet, etc.) and use these in a fictional composition.
4. Pupils can exchange stories and underline what they think may be a fact woven into the story. Check with the author to see if they are right.

■ Correlating science lessons with other areas of the curriculum, current events, etc. is nothing new. Yet there are some *events, holidays, and special weeks,* that are overlooked but which offer a new twist to science.

• For example, at Christmas time, how many teachers give lessons on deciduous trees? or relate tree needles to leaves and make comparisons? or, brainstorming a bit, is there any science in Christmas tree ornaments? Of course—in the way they are made, how they are colored or silvered, how modern plastics have taken the place of glass.

• Let's turn attention to another "day" to capitalize on—Arbor Day. It varies from state to state, but whenever it occurs in your state, use the day to start teaching about plants. The average child's first contact with plants, trees, and bushes are those he sees around school or his own home. Most of these trees and bushes are "cultivars" plants that have been hybridized or bred for decorative use. Yet, few children are ever told any facts about them. Most are not probably native, but they are nevertheless one of a child's first contact with plants. A bush (a privet hedge or a yew or alpine currant) may be the first large outdoor plant a child may have fingered. Teach children about these in school! Later they can learn about wild plants. You might start in second grade with a series of lesson plans like this:

  1. Have a local gardener or greenhouse landscaper walk around the school grounds with you, pencil and paper in hand, and identify all the trees and shrubs. Make a map and mark locations.
  2. Almost all good greenhouses have card files of cultivated plants. Borrow these and get the scientific name

of each tree and shrub. Make a card on each one like
this:

Forsythia—Forsythia intermedia (Zabel.) also called golden bell.
A native hybrid (F. suspensa x F. viridissima) of China. It is hardy
and reaches an ultimate height of 8–10 feet with a spread of
10–12 feet. This type is different from other forsythias in that its
branches are more erect and do not droop as much.
In spring it is rich yellow, then yellow green; in winter it grad-
ually turns dull, to neutral yellow. The bark is smooth, yellowish.
It bears leaves from midspring to late fall; the leaves often are
3-parted. The flowers appear in early spring, before the leaves,
and are profusely produced. The fruit appears in late summer,
and are 2-valved capsules. Should be pruned after flowering
only. It should be thinned and renewed occasionally, cutting
3-year-old wood at the ground.

3. Make a map of the school grounds and number locations where bushes are found. Give one to each pupil,
   along with the names of plants with facts as shown
   above. Adjust the level of the material to suit your
   class.
4. Conduct a field trip around the grounds and have the
   pupils examine and identify the plants. Let them sit in
   a group on the ground while you tell facts or point
   out shapes or leaves, height, etc. (Incidentally, for
   lower grade pupils, this is an excellent introduction to
   map study!) If you can, let them take samples of the
   leaves and have them make a leaf booklet with common names, scientific names, etc. Use two or three
   days to complete the trip if necessary.
5. Covers can be made for the booklets. Making some
   kind of medal or a ribbon, give each child an award
   to wear after the study, to show they are now "registered school botanists."

- You can "brainstorm" other holiday science lessons. But try to
  include activities for the students. Don't be afraid to let the pupils
  do the investigations. This provides for individual differences, too.
  Science can do much to develop "doing-skills" in children, such
  as:
     (1) carrying out experiments with equipment at hand;
     (2) determining importance of information, what infor-
         mation is needed and if there is enough information;
     (3) comparing likenesses and differences;
     (4) observing and reporting phenomena; and
     (5) deciding on the most efficient way to get needed in-
         formation or data.

■ *One bag of tricks* to engage pupils in activity with a lot of science background is to use bags! Assemble several large paper bags for group work. In each one put a different variety of objects from which something can be made. For example, put in some gears, a metal rod, rubber bands, clips, brads, tape and small pieces of cardboard.

- Have a group take a bag, then tell them what they are to make from the materials in their bag. (With the gears, rod, etc. you might tell them to make a working toy.) Have the group compose a short paper giving the scientific principles involved in their project and explaining *why* it works. This may be used as a culminating activity after the study of physical principles. The "ingenuities" might be put on display at science fairs.

■ *Measurement* is one of the skills that a scientist uses. Usually results of measurement are tabulated or put into graph form. Students should be given practice in graphing results, for one of the best ways for young minds to see the results of experiments is through graphs. Each student or group of students can quickly make a re-usable graph with string and some map pins. If you use a bulletin board covered with plain paper the coordinates can be marked quickly with felt pen. To make a line graph the map pins can be stuck into the board with colored string or yarn, wound once around the first pin and the string carried to the next pin, wound around it, carried to the next pin, and so on. Two or more results can be plotted on the same coordinates by using different colored strings for each. In this way the entire class or group can view the graphs and comparisons are quickly seen.

■ *Experiments* (which would be more correctly called "experiences") are usually associated with science. Students love to do things, for they like to see for themselves. One of the most anticipated fields of science is that of chemistry. It is not easy for teachers to find good chemistry experiences. Many of them are risky. When, however, they are done for the class by the teacher, *she*, the teacher, has all the experience—and all the fun! If a teacher properly prepares the class so that "laboratory behavior" is clearly understood the class can be broken down into groups of the teacher's selection.

- Beforehand (with the aid of pupils, if the teacher likes) she can prepare show boxes of equipment which each group will use and be responsible for. (Washing and keeping equipment in order is as much of a science as are the learned facts teachers usually test.)
- Issue the shoe box to each group with a check list of the materials that are included, as stated on the sheet. (If they do not know

the names of the materials, they will ask and learn better than if
you told them!)
- For the experiments which follow, these materials were included
  in each box: four test tubes, paper towels, test tube brush, test
  tube rack, graduates, evaporating dishes, envelopes, a small quantity of citric acid, baking soda, two iron nails and zinc pellets.
- On a reagent "shelf" solutions of copper sulfate, sodium chloride,
  silver nitrate, potassium chromate and lead acetate were placed
  for students to use as needed. The "shelf" can be any table, but
  label it the "reagent table." Before the students begin, the teacher
  should explain what a reagent shelf is and the proper method of
  pouring chemicals from bottles to test tubes. *Be sure to include
  the fact that acid should always be poured into water and water
  (or solutions) should never be poured into acids.*

With the proper teaching, instructors will have no trouble allowing students
to do the following experiments. The author has used these with many
classes with complete success. The experiments were bound into "dittoed"
pamphlet form for each pupil to use. Pupils wrote directly into the pamphlets and had each experiment checked before proceeding to the next one.
Basic tests were used for reference and additional reference materials were
placed on a "reference shelf."

1. Place a piece of zinc in a test tube and add 5 ml of dilute HCl.
Feel the test tube bottom.
- What is the symbol for zinc? (Teacher can post a periodic table
  in the room for reference.)
- What is HCl?
- What does the prefix "hydro-" mean?
- What evidence of a reaction do you observe?
- What is meant by a "reaction" here?
- What gas do you think is being produced?
- Why do you think so?
- What form of energy appears to be associated with this reaction?
Set the test tube in the rack and let the reaction continue until no gas
forms. In the meantime continue with the following.
2. Pour 3 ml of copper sulfate into a test tube. Drop in (*Gently!!*)
an iron nail. After a while remove the nail and examine the portion
that was immersed in the copper sulfate.
- What is your observation? (Let the pupil tell you—don't tell him
  what is supposed to happen. Remember, observation should include more than visual examination: students should include the
  observation that heat was not or was evolved—or that an odor
  was or was not given off.)
- Explain what you think happened.
- Can you write an equation telling what happened? (Be sure your
  references cover this. Serve as a resource and conduct an appro-

priate lesson on writing equations. Do not underestimate the abilities of upper grade pupils here. This can be eliminated with lower grade pupils.)

3. Pour 5 ml of NaCl solution in a tube and add a few drops of silver nitrate solution.

- What happened?
- What do you see?
- Explain what you think happened?

4. To 5 ml of lead acetate solution in a test tube add equal volumes of potassium chromate solution.

- Feel the tube. What do you feel?
- What do you observe?
- What is a "precipitate?"
- What does a precipitate form? (The word precipitate is used here without explanation. In this way students must use references. The teacher should serve as a guide in doing these experiments.)

5. Now go back to No. 1. Place 2 or 3 ml of the solution in an evaporating dish and evaporate to dryness. (Have alcohol lamps available to do this. To prevent accidents, the author usually stationed himself at the table with the burners to supervise in compliance with state laws. Incidentally, some states require that students wear safety glasses. Be sure you know your state law!)

- What do you see in the dish? Describe what you see. (The material in the dish is zinc chloride formed when the zinc took the place of hydrogen in HCl and formed zinc chloride.)
- How many new substances were formed by this reaction?

6. Add dry citric acid to some baking soda in a test tube. Hold the thumb over the open end and shake. Now add 5 ml of water.

- Did anything happen when the chemicals were dry?
- What happened when the water was added?
- What does this show about the behavior of chemicals?

7. Hold a piece of magnesium ribbon in a pair of tongs. Hold at arm's length in the flame of a burner.

- Does a chemical reaction take place?
- How do you know?
- What is the white substance made of?

All the above experiments are simple and easy. It should be kept in mind that the pacing of the class is very important. In some classes each experiment should be followed by class discussion, reading, checking, and questioning. In fact, these can be used as a basis for a team teaching effort with several teachers working together, one preparing explanations in large group sessions, another supervising the "lab."

If you do not have enough lab tables, ordinary desks can be converted into large working surfaces with plywood overlays. Four desks can be put together and fitted with a piece of plywood, slightly larger, to make one working surface to accommodate a group. Strips of wood on the underside of the plywood can be used to hold the wood in place. These surfaces are flat, removable for easy storage and take up a minimum of space.

■ If you have pupils do experiments—whether they are repeats of what the books say or experiments of your own choosing—and you require them to write up their experiments, let the *written work* follow a more meaningful pattern than the typical " problem, procedure, materials used, experiment, and conclusion" set-up. In problem-solving, whether in science or math or in everyday living, the procedure we all go through is the same. For example, if you ask someone to get you a drink of water, the person who is asked is confronted with the problem of getting what you want. It may sound simple, but look! The person must understand your request—he must understand the problem. Then he must gather facts, such as thinking of where the water supply is, what containers are available, what must be done to get the glass to you. Under ordinary circumstances this can be done quickly and efficiently—but only because the person has facts! If your request is put to someone who is not familiar with the surroundings or conditions, he must consume more time to solve the problem because he must gather the facts. When students do experiments, you like for them to do some thinking—to show that they have done so, ask them to write up their experiments in the following form:

1. STATEMENT OF PROBLEM

   Be sure they understand what the problem says. You might have them put the problem in their own words, or discuss it with the class to establish its exact meaning.

   Suppose the problem is, "Do the roots of plants always tend to grow down and the stems up?" Discussion with the class should establish that the problem covers only those plants with roots and stems, and that such plants are generally the green ones with which they are familiar.

2. GATHERING OF FACTS

   The pupils should gather all the facts that *they think* will have bearing on the solution. Let them put down the facts they think are important. Don't eliminate any unless you know the fact to be erroneous. (The author likes to have students distinguish at this point the facts they have learned in school or from books and the facts they know from their own experience.)

   Continuing with the above problem as an illustration, students might list as a fact from experience that the plants they have seen have roots in the ground and stems above the ground.

3. HYPOTHESIS

   This is the experiment, based on facts, that will be planned and that the pupil thinks will give him the answer to the problem. In the illustration given above, the author had many variations of plants growing upside down. Some of the brighter students started with quick-sprouting seeds grown in jars or tumblers held against the inside of the glass with damp blotters. These were easily managed and were easily turned upside down and back again to right side up, etc.!

4. EXPERIMENT
   The pupil outlines what he has done and records his observations in whatever form he chose. Measurements are encouraged.

5. CONCLUSION
   The precision of stating a conclusion should be discussed with the students. Over-concluding should be discussed. The wise use of such phrases as "From this experiment . . . ," "Under the conditions used here . . ." or "Using the materials as described above . . ." should be stressed. Students should also know that for experiments to be valid, they must be repeated over and over again. If experiments are carried out in groups with each group doing the same, results from all groups can be considered as having been repetitions of the same.

This same form for "writing up" experiments can be used as a format for science fairs.

■ Field trips are, and should be, taken by science classes. If you take your class to an arboretum or on some other nature "hike," take along a microscope or two. Many of the new lightweight student zoom microscopes manufactured today are easy to carry. A small box with some slides, an eye-dropper, a single edged razor blade can be carried as adjuncts. To get pond water to stay on a slide, a depression slide is the best, but if you do not have one, take some vaseline along and with a pencil or toothpick make a shallow ring to hold the pond water.

- Leaves can be split, to get thin membranous epidermal tissue. With this placed on a slide, students have a fresh preparation of plant cells to view.
- If pupils on the trip want to collect leaves, take along some newspaper in a heavy manila folder or envelope to serve as a kind of temporary botanical press. Leaves are held flat this way for later mounting in glass.

There is absolutely no reason why the teaching of science should not be a highpoint of each day that you teach it!

Use These for Enrichment:

Blough, Glenn O. and Marjorie Campbell. *Making and Using Classroom Science Materials in the Elementary School.* New York: Dryden Press Inc., 1954.

Burnett, Will. *Teaching Science in the Elementary School.* New York: Rinehart & Co., Inc., 1953.

Hennessy, David E., *Elementary Teacher's Classroom Science Demonstrations & Activities.* West Nyack, N.Y.: Parker Publishing Company, Inc., 1964.

Nelson, Pearl Astrid, *Science Activities for the Younger Child.* West Nyack, N.Y.: Parker Publishing Company, Inc., 1968.

Syrocki, John B. *Science Activities for the Elementary Grades.* West Nyack, N.Y.: Parker Publishing Company, Inc., 1968.

UNESCO. Source Book for Science Teaching. France: UNESCO, 1962.

14

Science: Flexibility Through Independent Study

Joseph H. Caldwell

> *If I were to ask one thing above all others of elementary teachers, it would be imagination—the kind of mind that is playful, fanciful, odd in the relationships it perceives, that actively connects things as they are with things as they might be, that always pokes into corners and comes up with that which excites laughter or wonder.*
>
> *Kenneth Eble*

ABOUT THE AUTHOR

Joseph Caldwell received his Bachelor of Science and Master of Science degrees from Florida State University. He was selected for the 1964–65 Academic Year Institute at the University of Florida, a year of graduate study sponsored by the National Science Foundation. He completed the Specialist in Education degree in Curriculum and Instruction at the University of Florida. He has taught the 4th through the 8th grades in both departmentalized and self-contained classrooms and was principal of Mill Creek School, St. Johns County, Florida. His fields are science, math and guidance. Mr. Caldwell was co-author of the book, *The Come-Alive Classroom.* He is presently with the Florida Junior College at Jacksonville as the Director of Student Services for its San Diego and Southside Campuses.

Until quite recently the development of the elementary program in science enjoyed little of the emphasis that has been found at the secondary level. In establishing an adequate science program we are faced with a task becoming more difficult. As the scientific body of knowledge continues to mushroom and the range of sophistication of the elementary science student increases the difficulty becomes even more acute.

A method which could be of assistance to the teacher involves considerable independent study and individual exploration. Too often the upper elementary student's interest is stifled by a forced review of science material he has covered previously while no provision is made for deepening his knowledge in the field.

If we encourage the student's individual exploration in the field of science —that is to a significant degree to discover for himself through independent or small group effort—problems of individual motivation and those of work on the student's educational level may be reduced. The student should be placed in the active role of investigating and discovering science from all sides. Within the general guidelines agreed upon by the student and teacher, the student should be actively involved in observing, identifying, interpreting, recording, discussing, and developing basic skills necessary to carry out his work and in general deepening his knowledge in various fields.

Another suggestion involves relating the students' science experiences to other subjects instead of teaching science as a separate entity. A carefully planned program of independent study with a proper system of evaluation can easily involve, not only the sciences but English, spelling, speech, art and mathematics. In fact, most—if not all—elementary school subjects can be included.

Any program of independent study should be carefully supervised by the teacher, particularly in its initial phase. This supervision will help insure:

1. Proper use of time.
2. Availability of resources to the student, either directly or as obtainable from outside sources.
3. That the student is attempting work on the level which he is able to operate.

In a program of this type, students spend time out of school, as well as class time, in the study of their selected problem or subject. At least one hour a week should be reserved for students to read, research, conduct experiments and generally receive guidance regarding their work. At this time, while some students are working independently (or perhaps with the help of classmates), the teacher confers with other students regarding their progress. The conference may involve such items as a particular problem with an experiment or plans for obtaining help from an expert in the field.

An additional period each week could be spent allowing selected students to report to the class on their experimental work or having them relate information regarding the subject they are studying. The student should be expected to:

      1. Make several explorations in one year.

      2. Evaluate his experiences

         a. orally to the class in terms of major findings.

         b. in writing to the teacher.

      3. Keep records of

         a. time spent in his efforts.

         b. sources explored.

The student should be allowed to select topics with teacher assistance. However, on some occasions the teacher may desire to assign a topic to the student. Work on alternate topics would be scheduled to coordinate with general science work being done in class throughout the year.

The teacher should post a record with each student's subjects and "due date" for project presentation. The form shown was found to be effective. It provides for two evaluations per week with one assigned subject and one the student has selected.

SPECIAL REPORTS				
Class: 6-Y				
Date	Student	Subject Assigned	Student	Subject Selected
Sept. 25	Brooker	Early Means of Communication Across Space ¡ Time	Hawks	Construction of Bridges
Oct. 2	Beckford	Telegraph and Semaphore	Thames	Native Rocks and Minerals
Oct. 9	Hunter	Telephone	Smith	Plant Life of Oceans
Oct. 16	McLatchey	Radio	Harris	Underwater Exploration

As the report day arrives the student should be reminded of the time schedule. All of his work must be brought together for presentation at the appropriate time.

Students should be encouraged to utilize visual aids and the production of such material should be considered an integral part of the program.

Associated with the actual presentation, the use of a tape recorder is valuable in providing:

1. The student a record of his presentation for self-evaluation.
2. A record of better reports for use as examples.
3. A source of review for students who have been absent. (This works well when equipment is outfitted with an earphone plug which silences external speakers.)

As part of the learning situation the student should be advised early in the year that evaluation, while it may be primarily in terms of science, will involve other subject areas. It may include appropriate English, spelling, artwork (as needed) and the ability to orally communicate the results of his work.

In departmentalized situations, some science teachers have found their English teaching colleagues willing to criticize the science student's work in terms of grammar and composition. The language arts teacher may be willing to allow credit in English for the student's effort!

The science teacher and student should jointly evaluate the work within a short time following presentation. When grading written reports, the teacher can attach an evaluation sheet for use in later discussions.

GUIDE FOR REPORTING YOUR WORK

Make your report interesting. Tell about things you would be interested in hearing. The purpose of the report includes helping others to think about the subject. When a person is interested, he will probably ask questions. You should be prepared to answer general questions about your subject.

If you write for information, make sure you allow 2-3 weeks for an answer.

Reports may be written in pen or pencil. You should be very careful to use correct English and spelling.

On the last page list the references you used (books, places to which you wrote for information, interviews, conferences, etc.)

In addition to any visual material, it is often helpful to use the chalkboard to draw diagrams or to use models to help people to understand your subject better.

You will be graded on the following:

How well you covered the subject as originally planned:	60 points
English and spelling:	15 points
Presentation:	5 points
Visual aids or project:	10 points
How well you answer general questions:	<u>10 points</u>
	100 points

There is little excuse for failure to have your report ready. You will know the date for presentation well in advance. If for some very important reason, you cannot give your report, let me know the day before you are to present it.

If you need to change a subject or an experiment, see me and we will discuss the change.

EVALUATION SHEET

SCIENCE REPORT

Name: **George McLatchey**

Class: **6-Y**   Date: **Oct. 16**

Item	Score Poss.	Score Revd.
Subject Coverage	60	**58**
English and Spelling	15	**6**
Presentation	5	**4**
Visual or Project	10	**10**
Answering Questions	10	**8**

Total: 100   **86**

Comments: **You did a good job of covering the subject. Still need work on English and Spelling. Project quite interesting.**

Working with students in an independent study system will call for different and often unique methods of communication. While reviewing written materials in the science field in book or periodical form you might uncover an article of importance to one or several students. However, it may be one of little concern to the whole class. There is a temptation to utilize regular class time and involve the entire group with such material. A system found useful in this case incorporates a route slip similar to those used in business.

The teacher attaches this slip to a copy of the article and at the same time checks the name of the students, under the column headed "To," that he feels could use or would be interested in the information. Students read, initial, comment (if they desire) and pass the information on to the next student on the list.

As an assist to yearly planning, as well as the assignment of topics and experiments, a projected annual schedule is of help.

This serves as a broad plan to draw together areas in science that are covered in the regular program, materials needed, and related student projects.

Resources available to the students should be stressed. Too often teachers feel limited to the school library when referring students for information.

B-2   TIMES-UNION AND JOURNAL, JACKSONVILLE, SUNDAY, JUNE 30, 1968

C.S. LONG LINES TO LAY 1,200 MILES OF PHONE CABLE

Ship Here to Put Virgin Isles on Dial

By JOHN LEACH
Times-Union Staff Writer

The CS Long Lines is lying heavily at anchor here, 1,100 miles of telephone cable resting in her hold, ready to connect Jacksonville and other cities by wire with the Virgin Islands.

The ship is the most sophisticated of its kind, and was specially made for laying transoceanic cable.

Capt. James Connelly is skipper of the 17,000-ton vessel.

SHIP'S BOW THREADS OUT CABLE

VISITORS ON TOUR OF SHIP VIEW CABLE FEED DRUM

—TIMES-UNION PHOTOS BY RAY STAFFORD

CAPT. CONNELLY IN PILOT ROOM

ROUTE SLIP

Article: *Ship To Put Virgin Isles On Dial*

Comment: *This article has information related to your work on Communication. You might call Mr. Hayes. He attended the Open House Saturday and took pictures.*

Name	To	Init.	Comment	Name	To	Init.	Comment
Jack	✓			Janet	✓		
Bobby				Jean			
Ivan				Nancy			
Kent				Peggy	✓		
Ronnie				Mary			
Rod				Jenny			
Ramsey				Linda			
George	✓			Faye			
Alex				Gail			
Eric				Patsy			
Sandy							
Jim							
Joe							

PROJECTED ANNUAL SCHEDULE					Class: 6-Y
Week & Date	Coverage		Audio-Visual Aids	Books & Other Aids	Student Reports Assigned
	Description	Text Pages			
1 Oct. 2	Man's Early Methods of Communication.	8-35	Development of Communicat. (Univ.-87143)	Beginnings of Communication- Smith	Brooker-Early Means of Communication Across Time & Spc. Hawks- Const. Bridge
2 Oct. 9	Methods of Communication Across Space	36-50	How Teleg. Works (Univ.-82146) Use of Codes	Samuel Morse, Inventor - Brown	Beckford- Telegraph and Semaphore Thames- Native Rocks and Minerals
3 Oct. 16	Telephones and Dial Switching Systems	51-70	Electricity and Commun. (Univ.-15711) *Check with Phone Co.	Alexander G. Bell - Harper	Hunter- The Telephone Smith- Plant Life of the Ocean

Little thought is given to parents whose occupation or training is in science or to local doctors, nurses, mechanics, artists and others with science-related backgrounds.

Take advantage of factories, equipment and projects that can be visited by class representatives who will report to the class.

Professional persons and technicians are usually glad to interview students studying a subject related to their field. Where an entire class is too large, a single student visits and returns with information.

High school and college students are a good source of help for after-school field work.

At times it may not be feasible to organize field trips or visits to obtain information on a scientific subject. Often the facilities involved cannot accommodate groups of normal class size. In cases of this type, serious consideration should be given to arranging a visit between the student and an expert. While it may not be possible for a doctor to interview an entire class in a medical lab, he may be willing to spend a bit of time with a student or a small group explaining, for example, how X-ray photographs are made, how blood is typed or what is involved in treating a person bitten by a rabid dog. Valuable information thus obtained can be brought back to the classroom by a student's first-hand experience.

The suggestions made in this chapter are but a few designed to initiate a program of independent study. As you work with this type program, short cuts for more efficient organization of your program will become apparent.

$$15$$

We Were There: Social Studies Through Experiences

Virginia R. Beaty

ABOUT THE AUTHOR

Virginia Beaty received the Bachelor of Arts degree from Redlands University in Redlands, California, and has completed an additional 56 hours of graduate work. She has traveled in Mexico, Canada and through the New England and Pacific Coastal states. She has taught in the elementary school for 25 years and is presently with the Santa Monica, California school system.

The whole point of social studies in the elementary school must be to involve children in society: its peoples, its roles, its geography, its needs, economics and services. Not reading *about* but *living through* as many experiences as possible.

In Social Studies we study how man, innately gregarious, has worked out the problem of living together for his own protection, to satisfy his personal needs of food, clothing and shelter, to organize into groups to form social institutions (churches and schools), social legislation and all types of cooperative and interdependent relationships such as in transportation, in his daily labor for his livelihood and in his leisure time activities. In all of this social organization man sometimes finds that his personal freedom has disappeared. Some governments consider this loss beneficial to the group as a whole. Other governments build the whole system of government around the value of the individual, the individual having the right to vote for his leaders and his behavioral laws and benefits. The comparison is vital in Social Studies.

For children to want to learn, they must become involved in an intense relationship with the subject. As one can see, the Social Studies program is rich with creative possibilities, for the fun of Social Studies *is* its involvement. The question the teacher should continually ask himself is, "What can I do, what can I find, what can I bring to the class that would make countries—or situations—and their people come to life for my students?" How can the teacher, as Lillian Smith expressed it, "turn on lights in imaginations"?

BUILDING BACKGROUND FOR A UNIT

Stimulating interest and setting the proper mood for a unit is very important. Building a background may be done with a group first and then individually. Together—with map and globe we decide:

a. What continent, what country, what state is it in?

b. The area is bordered by what country, what ocean, river, state?

c. It is north, south, east and west of what?

d. What is its location with respect to the equator or Poles and how would this determine climate?

e. What type of terrain does it have—mountains, rivers, lakes, coastline, desert, jungle?

The following films are very helpful:

Maps and Their Meaning: 14 min. 1950 4–6 Academy Films

Maps are explained as symbols of geographical information. The color zones on physical maps are illustrated by the types of land found in each zone. Animated maps, diagrams, and color photography point out various economic aspects of altitude, latitude and rainfall, especially the ways in which they effect the use of the land.

Maps Are Fun: 10 min. 1946 4–6 Coronet Films

Introduces the fundamental concepts of map reading and includes the principles of scale, symbols, physical and political maps with various uses of color. Also, how to use a map index.

Maps: (Coastal Symbols and Terms) 14 min. 1957 4–6 Academy Films

Explains and visualizes symbols and terms used on maps, describing and locating land and water formations along 4,900 miles of U.S. coastline. Includes the terms coastline, bays, harbor, peninsula, cape, island, lagoon, river mouth, delta, and gulf. Follows coastal formations through Boston Harbor, Bridgeport, Conn., New York Harbor, Mississippi River Delta

Region, New Orleans, the coast of Texas, and the Pacific coast at Los Angeles and San Francisco.

Maps: (Land Symbols and Terms) 14 min. 1956 4–6 Academy Films

Air views and photographs of representative areas of the United States are used in explaining how to interpret land symbols and terms which appear in map legends. Shows how the following are indicated on a map: cities of various sizes, state capitals, boundary lines, highways, deserts, national parks, waterfalls, canals, railroads, rivers and mountain peaks.

Maps: Where Am I? 11 min. 1963 K–6 Charles Cahill Co.

Begins with a floor plan of a house and a low aerial view of a section of a town and relates these to maps as pictures of the land.

Once the area is pinpointed and films, filmstrips and photographs have helped it become real, major divisions for individual work might include:

a. *Locating Areas on a Large Map*
   1. Find and mark with colored string or pins all points we located during group work.
   2. Find your own state. Find where you live now.
   3. Print your name on a piece of paper and pin it up to locate the town where you were born. (Have a box of pins and paper ready.)
      NOTE: All of this can be taken down two or three times to afford many turns during the week.

b. *Methods of Transportation*
   Methods of transportation suitable for the area and the period can be a research project.
   1. Use small pictures of uniform size and place in appropriate areas to depict:
      a. Water travel—rafts, canoes, ships on rivers, harbors, oceans.
      b. Land travel—mountains, deserts, plains with people traveling on foot and in carts pulled by man, wagons pulled by animals, and motorized travel using cars, trucks, trains and airplanes.
   2. Colored strings might be used to show the extent of travel at that time, using blue for the water, brown for the land and white for the air. This will also show the advancement of civilization.

c. *Products and Industries*
   After extensive viewing, reading and class discussion, children are ready to consider the products (natural and synthetic) and the industries of the area and the period.
   1. All of this lends itself to making wonderful pictorial maps. Each child is given a clearly outlined map on which the rivers and main cities have been drawn. He can draw or cut out and paste on:

✓ products and industries
✓ buildings
✓ transportation methods
✓ mountains, deserts, forests, plains, etc.

You probably have had numerous ideas along this line by now, but let's explore France, Switzerland and India for specifics.

FRANCE

There are many good films and books on French city and country life. For top reading groups *The Junior Britannica* has good material. Excellent pictures of Basque shepherds, fishing in Britanny, farming and cattle raising have been found in *Holiday* and *The National Geographic Magazine*. Many short songs and dance numbers enhance the study. *Sur Le Pont D'Avignon* and *Alouette* are found in many class songbooks. The album SONGS IN FRENCH FOR CHILDREN, with accompanying summaries to convey the sense of the lyrics, is fun to use. Beautiful posters showing the magnificent cathedrals of France are free for the asking from travel bureaus.

A compass rose (found on navigation charts) is used to establish geographical information. Many geographical terms become necessary and meaningful, such as:

Bay of Biscay on the *West*
English *Channel* on the *north*
Alps—*mountains* on the *east*
Pyrennees—mountains—*border* between Spain and France
Mediterranean *Sea* on the *southeast*
Countries of Belgium and Germany—on the *north*
Spain on the *southwest*
The Seine *River* runs *east* and *north*
Paris, the *capital city*, on the Seine

Using a French Tour Guide offers lots of fun. Find actual pictures of points of interest in Paris (Notre Dame, Eiffel Tower, boating on the Seine, sidewalk cafes, art displays and galleries) perfume from French factories, fashion books from the dress designing businesses. Place the pictures and objects in stationary areas and choose a guide to lead a group on a geographical tour. To vary this, a guide could take the group through and people could be stationed at each point of interest to give short, explanatory talks. Small groups could be brought through at spaced intervals to give more children a chance to be "guide."

"On The Streets of Paris" has been effectively used as a culmination of the study. Chairs and tables were casually grouped around three sides of the room like a sidewalk cafe.

Parisian visitors rest at a sidewalk cafe after a vigorous round of folk dancing.

1. *Art Show*: One committee prepared a series of pictures by French artists. Pictures were hung back of the tables, on the inside and outside of the room. Two or three children (in berets) conducted a casual tour and gave background on the pictures. The art show was followed by:

2. *A Puppet Show*: Another committee dramatized an original story with simple paper bag puppets. (These could be papier mâché or any kind you have time to make.) Students used *Le Petit Train* from SONGS IN FRENCH FOR CHILDREN for their background music and sound effects.

3. *Folk Dancing*: Then followed a dance to *Sur Le Pont D'Avignon*. The girls wore full skirts (for easy curtsying) and the boys with black paper mustaches and cardboard guns portrayed soldiers. Everyone sang as it was performed.

4. *Food*: A committee with white crepe paper aprons served a paper plate to each table with buttered French bread, small pieces of cheese and small apple sections. Grape juice, representing the French vineyards, was the beverage.

FILMS

Food for Paris Markets: 20 min. black and white 1949 United World Films

How large cities depend upon rural hinterlands to supply them with food is the lesson represented in this film. Fortunately, Paris can be reached easily from all parts of France. France is one of the Western European countries which has achieved a large degree of self-sufficiency in food supply.

Modern France, The Land and the People: 10 min. 1950 Color— Coronet Films. el-jh

An overall tour of France from the wheat fields of Normandy to Paris and the barges on the Seine. People and industries are included; also shots of steel workers, boatmen, grapegrowers, fishermen and truck gardeners.

BOOKS

Young France, by Leon A. Harris, Dodd, Mead and Co., 1964.
Getting to Know France, by John A. Wallace, Coward-McCann, 1962.

SWITZERLAND

The study of Switzerland offers an excellent opportunity to use a relief map—a molded plastic map where you can actually feel and see the mountains. Group study will probably bring out the fact that the country is *landlocked*. Count the many nationalities and languages involved in this tiny area—why is this so? Find an old copy of *William Tell* with the whole story of Switzerland's history. It gives a good understanding of the strong united spirit that exists in spite of natural barriers. (The exciting battle when William Tell and his brigands trapped Giesler and the mounted nobles in the canyon below inspired a spectacular painting lesson. What a tangle of horses, crossbows and blood!)

To appreciate and understand the country and village life of a growing Switzerland, use the following films and books which take you from old to new modern Switzerland.

FILMS

Village of Switzerland: 11 min. 1965 4–6 Churchill Films

This film is designed first of all to bring to life the Swiss people and their culture. It considers how a nation with virtually no natural

resources is able to have a high standard of living. It also explores the unique position of a small country surrounded by powerful neighbors which has maintained its freedom by an armed neutrality.
Switzerland, The Land and the People: 11 min. 1963 4–6 jh-sh Coronet

This film is an illustration of modern Switzerland including: grazing, lumbering, watchmaking, tourist industries in mountains, farming, manufacturing in Millelland region, banking, and commerce in Zurich, Berne, and Basel.

BOOKS

The Magic Meadow by Ingrid Aulaire, Doubleday, 1958.
Heidi by Johanna Spyri, Macrae Smith 1925 (original).
High in the Mountains by Emma Brock, Whitman, 1938.
Alpine Paths by Mildred H. Comfort, Beckley-Cardy, 1953.
Getting to Know Switzerland by Patricia Lauber, Coward-McCann, 1960.
Stories of William Tell and His Friends by H. E. Marshall, Dutton and Co., 1907.

Why is Switzerland so modern and affluent today? First and foremost, it has capitalized on tourist trade. It is easier to travel through the country now. Additionally, comfortable lodges, the best ski runs in the world, the best mountain climbing, great natural beauty, trained guides, modern weather warnings, excellent craftsmen, cosmopolitan people with many languages and the world bank—all these are reasons for Switzerland's prosperity.

Use the SOUND OF MUSIC story with its *Edelweiss song*. Bring in songs of the Alps with examples of yodeling.

As a treat, have a Swiss chocolate surprise one afternoon.

INDIA

The study of India is an especially good time for making a pictorial map because the Indians raise so many interesting products; sugar cane, rice, teak wood, tea, rubber and jute.

Many wild animals inhabit the land: elephants, tigers, monkeys, crocodiles, poisonous snakes, constrictors, camels, etc. The terrain is varied, too: jungle, river deltas, dry plateaus, and high mountains.

- As an art activity use large sheets of paper to illustrate the different animals. Have a variety of materials for the children to use: paint, chalk, cloth, colored papers, buttons, yarns, odds and ends to be glued to the animals.

• Plant and harvest a crop of rice in a rhythmical, graceful drama. Use pumps (long sticks and brooms) to water the field. Stoop and plant each shoot. Cut with a sickle. Pound the grains in hollowed out logs with a big wooden mallet to clean off the outside skin. "Water buffalos" haul the crop away to be stored in large clay jars (as tall as a third grader).

Children plant and harvest a crop of rice in a rhythmical, graceful drama.

• Let your students cook a pot of curry:

Real curry is not made with creamed sauce, so you might like to mix either tuna or chicken with rice and a small amount of curry powder. Around this have small bowls of salted peanuts, chutney, coconut, cut celery and cut pepper to eat with the curry. Each child could be responsible for bringing a food to help with the meal.

A standby that most children like is Tuna Curry:

This involves:

    2 cans condensed Cream of Mushroom soup

    1½ cups of water

    1⅓ cups quick cooking rice

    2 cups tuna

    1 cup chopped bell pepper

    1–2 teaspoons curry powder

    1 teaspoon salt

    dash of pepper

    1 cup chopped chives

    1 cup diced blanched almonds (optional)

    1 small can chopped pimento (optional)

    Mix soup and water, bring to boil. Add rice, tuna, celery, bell pepper, curry, salt, and bring to boiling point again. reduce heat, cover and let cook for 15 minutes. Add olives, almonds, and pimento just a few minutes before removing from heat. Serves 8.

● Do some weaving: Design woven samples that could be used for saris.

Give each child a paper base to weave on.

Have strips of many different colors and widths. Check pictures of saris to see how many colors are used. Have gold and silver strands available, too, if possible. Make the strands narrow as you come to the edge, just like the border on a sari.

● Invite an Indian student from a nearby college to speak, or a person from the community that has visited India. Ask them to demonstrate how to put on a sari properly. Supply cloth the right length and width for girls to practice putting on saris. Any bright cheap cloth could be used. Have a full length mirror for viewing, if possible.

FILMS

The Ganges River: 1955 el-sh McGraw Hill

Explains the religious and economic significance of the Ganges River. Traces the Ganges River from its source in the Himalayas to the Bay of Bengal. Shows many Hindus making the difficult month-long religious pilgrimage to the source of the river. Includes scenes showing how water from the sacred river is used in the wedding festival of a rajah.

Hindu Family: 10 min. 1952 4–6 Encyclopedia Brittanica Film Co.

A presentation of the family life of a Hindu village headman, centering around the forthcoming marriage of the oldest daughter. The everyday relaxations and work of the people of Atgaum in the province of Gujerat are depicted, as are various family relationships and religious practices.

India and Her Food Problem: 16 min. 1966 Primary-Elem. Atlantis Prod.

The future of India depends on her ability to increase the food supply faster than the increase of her population. Climate and altitude largely control where certain foods can be grown in India.

Story of Rice: 12 min. 1952 jh-c Encyclopedia Brittanica.

This film demonstrates modern methods of growing and marketing rice. It shows seeding of the fields by drill and by airplane, training and flooding of the fields, harvesting of the crop, drying and cleansing of the kernels, and the final polishing and packaging for market.

BOOKS

Uttam, A Boy of India by G. Warren Schloat Jr., Knopf, 1963.

Getting to Know the River Ganges by Welthy H. Soni, Coward-McCann, 1964.

Getting to Know India by Barnett D. Laschever, Coward, McCann, 1960.

SPECIAL ACTIVITIES

Learning about social studies, or any subject for that matter, is greatly enhanced by being able to touch, handle, try on, work with, use and figure out the artifacts of a country or period.

Artifacts and special activities may be used to introduce a unit or their use may be delayed until a good understanding of the material has been established. However, the fun in this type of learning is the independent activity. Think of—

a. Comparing the old with the new:
   1. Hour glass—stop watch
   2. Sun Dial—magnetic needle lying on a cork floating in water
b. Panning for gold by using a box of fine gravel, a box of fine sand, a pitcher of water and a gold pan (a shallow wash basin). This activity is best done outdoors. (I had an old prospector come to the classroom and show us the motion involved in panning.)

c. Balancing a papier mâché water jug on one's head (during a study of Indians, the nomad countries, etc.)

d. Demonstrating the steps involved in planting rice.

e. Trying on clothes of different countries: berets, turbans, Tyrolean hats, pioneer hats and bonnets, long full skirts, lederhosen, sarongs, saris. (A full length mirror and a place to stroll is helpful.)

f. Grinding grain with a grinding stone and metals (grinding bowl).

g. Making an adobe brick with straw, adobe (dry clay), water, a wooden frame and mixing box.

h. Conducting the business of a country store:
   1. Balance a 2 or 5 lb. sack of sugar with a weight.
   2. Barter with flour, sugar (sacks stuffed with paper)
      fresh farm vegetables (or plastic ones)
      eggs (just the cartons would do)
      bacon, beef jerky
      bread (labeled homemade)

i. Bargaining—as in a Mexican market

j. Holding an auction for furniture or land

k. Using the Viewmaster and reels, the viewer and slides, or the previewer and filmstrips to gain an understanding of the people, their costumes, shelter, work, schools, play, food, religion, terrain and their geographical position on the globe in relation to ours.

Comb the film libraries, be on the alert for magazine and newspaper articles, search for people who have visited or lived in the country, state or area your class is studying. Ask the librarian to work up a list of fiction, non-fiction and travel books which relate to the area. Write for pamphlets, brochures, travel guides, posters and materials to supplement the text book.

Chapter 16, pages 171–173 lists the addresses of foreign offices and tourist bureaus around the world. Contact them for information and material.

The Humble Oil Company has a fine collection of 16mm-sound motion pictures. Many prizes have been awarded to these travelogs, documentaries and adventure subjects. Write for their film catalog:

Public Relations Department
Humble Oil & Refining Co.
Box 2180
Houston, Texas 77001

Material is everywhere, ideas for activities and experiences are all around you—enlist the aid of travel agents, government offices, librarians, and audio-visual experts and citizens of the community as you bring your social studies program to life in the classroom.

16

Bring Your Trip to the Classroom

Glenn B. Schroeder

ABOUT THE AUTHOR

Glenn Schroeder received his Bachelor of Science degree from the Oregon College of Education and Master of Education degree from the University of Oregon. While completing his doctorate in Elementary Administration at the University of New Mexico, he held a position as Curriculum Research Assistant for the Southwestern Cooperative Education Laboratory. In addition to having taught single and multiple grades in Oregon and in Germany, Mr. Schroeder was principal of an elementary and junior high school with the Dependents Schools in Germany. He has traveled extensively in Europe, Canada, Mexico and the Far East. He contributed material in social studies to the book, *The Come-Alive Classroom*. Dr. Schroeder is presently an assistant professor of Education Administration and the Associate Director of the Educational Service Bureau at Temple University in Philadelphia.

The most obvious and probably the most valuable adjunct to travel (after considering the pleasure and relaxation one derives from a change of scene) is the opportunity to obtain ideas and materials that relate to your educational tasks. Whether it is a trip to the County Fair or to Timbuktu, the imaginative educator, with proper preparation, should be able to capitalize upon the experience.

Proper preparation is one of the keys to success in any endeavor and is of maximum importance in travel. A friend of this writer once expressed the concept of preparation in somewhat algebraic terms as being P^6 or P to the sixth power. To paraphrase him, P^6—proper prior preparation prevents poor programs. This advice certainly is apropos for travel and cannot receive too much attention.

Formulate a travel plan with your classroom in mind. It will provide a framework for adequate coverage of the essential and related points but is flexible enough to provide for spontaneity and the unexpected. DO YOUR HOMEWORK!

WHEREVER YOU ARE GOING:

- Attempt to obtain a thorough working knowledge of the area concerning such factors as the history, the geography, the climate, the people and their customs, the economy, the politics, the usual as well as the unusual sights and other aspects peculiar or applicable to the area.
- If you are going to a non-English speaking country, learn a few phrases. Nothing will endear you to the hearts of the populace more than displaying an effort to greet them in their own language. Learning to say "Good morning" or "Good evening" is a fine start.
- If at all possible, seek out people who have been to the places where you contemplate traveling. Ask them about things of your interest. Also ask what they were most interested in when they were there. They can give you another perspective of the area. *A word of caution*: no two people see any one place in the same way. Make up your own mind about a place while you are there, not before you arrive!
- There are numerous other sources available for the study of your chosen area; many are readily available at your local public, school or college library. Others require a letter of inquiry.
- For those who would rather leave some of the planning to others, don't overlook the multitude of tours that are available. Reliable travel agents can arrange for your participation in a guided tour with a group or an individual itinerary complete with tickets and reservations just for you.
  - Educators might want to investigate the National Education Association sponsored tours. NEA members usually receive a discount. Some of these tours have college credit available and the tuition is included in the cost. For information:
    NEA Division of Educational Travel
    1201 16th Street, N.W.
    Washington, D.C. 20036

Relating Your Travel to the Classroom

Each individual will have to determine his own subject matter needs and choose the best way to relate his travel to the classroom. One must remember that when traveling, space as well as funds may be limited, therefore, quality, not quantity is the keynote.

What are some of the media that should be considered?

Heiligenblut, Austria. A small village at the southern end of the Grossglockenerhochalpenstrasse, an alpine pass between Austria and Germany.

PHOTOGRAPHY

● One should make an effort to develop skills in this area. It is not as difficult as you might imagine to master the mechanics of a good camera. Once this is done, you can concentrate on what is being exposed on the film. The average person can take pictures of good technical quality which is all that is necessary for instructional purposes. Develop your artistry later. Photography is highly satisfying and, besides, it is not possible to buy pictures of everything that could be used in the classroom or for one's own pleasure.

● Slides—Take abundant colored slides and buy only those that you need but cannot take yourself. Commercial slides that are sold in souvenir shops are usually not of good quality so select them *carefully*. Street hawkers will often barter slides for American cigarettes but the quality of the slides leaves much to be desired.

● Still pictures—Colored pictures can be reproduced from your slides if you can rely on a good company for the work. Black and white photos are excellent, inexpensive and can be enlarged very easily. Do it yourself, it's fun! Let your school's photography club enlarge some for you or work with the media production personnel of your school system to produce enlargements. The enlargements or the regular "drug store" size can be used in many ways, including:

    (1) on bulletin boards,
    (2) in scrapbooks,
    (3) mounted with captions for displays or as teaching aids,
    (4) writing your own textbook and illustrating it with pictures,
    (5) having the students write a text for the pictures as they relate to the particular topic of study.

What are some examples of things that you might photograph, either in black and white, color, or slides for educational use that would not necessarily be of personal interest?

    (1) crops in various stages of development
    (2) farm implements
    (3) transportation—land, air and water
    (4) types of architecture
    (5) geologic formations
    (6) types of buildings—schools, public offices, stores, factories, etc.

"Tipsy Tower" (Falterturn) of Kitzengen, Germany. Typical
of village towers of the 15th and 16th centuries.

(7) road signs

(8) industrial processes

● Motion pictures—Making good motion pictures is much more difficult
than taking still pictures. If you are skilled in this medium, decide what you
want and shoot it. The film can be edited and spliced for an effective presentation. The gaps left by the motion picture can be filled, or points that
need extra stress can be supplemented, by still pictures, or slides, color
or black and white.

● Equipment—Keep it simple and effective. This writer always carries
two cameras, one for 35 mm slides and one for 2¼″ x 2¼″ black and

City hall (Rathaus) of Alsfeld, Germany. An example of the half-timbered (Fachwerk) structures found in many areas of Europe, especially northern Germany.

white film. This procedure is recommended over attempting to take one roll of slides and alternate with one roll of black and white. Inevitably, one wants to use the type of film that is not in the camera. A happy compromise would be a good camera that employs interchangeable film magazines *a la Hasselblad*. For more information on photography, see Selected Bibliography I.

• Film—If you are going abroad, take a good supply of film with you. *Good* camera film is usually more expensive in other countries.

REALIA

This is another very important educational medium and traveling pre-

Statue of Hans Christian Anderson in Copenhagen, Denmark.

sents an excellent opportunity to "beef-up" your units with real materials. Some kinds of things that might fit into your classroom work are:

- Art work in various media
- Mineral and rock samples
- Unusual tools
- Children's toys and school material
- Postage stamps and coins
- Dolls in unusual costumes
- Handicraft such as jewelry, textiles and so forth

PRINTED MATERIAL

Traveling also presents an opportunity to obtain supplemental materials

St. Basil's cathedral in Moscow's Red Square. It is now a
museum with an entrance fee of 20 kopecks (22¢).

for various and sundry teaching units; most of it would be free or very
inexpensive. This material can also be mailed to your home rather inexpensively as most countries have a special rate for books and educational
material.

Where do you find this material?

● Tourist information offices and commercial tour companies usually
have free brochures, maps, travel posters and booklets.

● Book or souvenir shops usually have a multitude of inexpensive
material concerning various aspects of the area you are visiting. *Don't overlook postcards* as a source of good pictures.

● Specialized shops, especially in countries that rely on vast amounts of
propaganda, sell posters inexpensively. In Moscow, for example, a small
government store sells nothing but books and huge propaganda posters. A

friend of this writer used some of these posters very effectively in communications and social studies units.

● Museums or other places that attract tourists usually have inexpensive materials available.

In almost any place in the world, this material can be obtained in English or in English and several other languages simultaneously.

VERBAL RECORDS

Do not overlook this aspect of traveling. The best of us forget impressions over a period of time unless we can refresh our memories in some way. Give some thought to how you, as an individual, might best keep a record for your particular purposes. The two basic methods of maintaining a verbal record are:

● Spoken—a small, battery-operated tape recorder of *high fidelity* is on the list of "nice to take" but is not essential, especially if you are limited in space or weight. Tapes can be mailed home when filled. With a tape recorder, one can record on-the-scene sounds and impressions as events or sights are viewed. The tapes can be edited and master tapes made after your return from the trip.

● Written—If you do not use tape, keep a *daily*, written journal of impressions, places, events, sights, people and so forth. Do not trust your memory for details. *Keep a daily log.*

Keeping a verbal record of your travels may seem to be a drudge at the time but you will certainly find that you can conjure up details that would otherwise be lost with the passage of time.

Other Possible Benefits Related to Travel

Besides the personal satisfaction, relaxation and the wealth of material and experiences one can bring to his educational task as a result of travel, other possibilities should not be overlooked.

● Speaking engagements or lectures—Do not forget these possibilities. Many clubs and organizations endeavor to find people who can present a program on travel. Beyond the personal satisfaction and public relations gained from this kind of activity, one is usually paid a small honorarium for speaking engagements. Plan well before traveling!

● Writing—Do not overlook the possibility of writing magazine articles, books, texts and other items of a journalistic nature. Good planning before the trip and good recording during the trip will greatly facilitate this enterprise.

This writer would be remiss in his function if he concluded without pointing out that, even with the best planning, the traveler's attitude will be a major factor in determining whether or not his trip is to be a success. Two people can go to the same places at the same time and have identical experiences; one will enjoy himself immensely, the other will be completely miserable. The differences are usually attributable to attitudes.

You cannot expect to have all of the comforts of your own home or be completely understood at all times. You *can* expect to encounter some difficulties. Accept difficulties philosophically, keep a positive attitude and *smile*. Your trip will be successful!

SELECTED BIBLIOGRAPHY

I. Photography

This bibliography is designed to help the reader, whether a novice or advanced photographer, locate some material that might prove helpful to him in any aspect of photography. The selections cover a spectrum from selecting a camera to processing your own color prints. This list is by no means exhaustive but represents the best of what was available for the writer to peruse. Considering the list in its entirety, the books by Feininger seem to be the best.

The listing of magazines is merely to help the reader determine some of the representative titles in photographic periodicals. *Peruse them closely at your newsstand or library before subscribing to any of them.*

BOOKS

Aston, Kevin L. *Candid Photographic Portraiture*. New York: American Photographic Book Publishing Co., Inc., 1965. 144 pp.
This book concerns itself with the photography of people in their life situations. Good source for someone who might photograph people while on a trip.
Feininger, Andreas. *The Complete Photographer*. Englewood Cliffs, New Jersey: Prentice-Hall, Inc., 1965. 344 pp.
The title of this book is definitely not misleading. The author says that his purpose is one of helping people become good photographers. A thorough perusal of this volume could not help but improve the interested person's technical skills. The detailed table of contents and index make the book very easy to use. As an added bonus, complete cross-references and illustrations are provided. Highly recommended for anyone's reference library if they own a camera. Very well written and practical.
Feininger, Andreas. *Total Picture Control, A Personal Approach to Photography*. New York: Crown Publishers, Inc., 1961. 351 pp.
Excellent for both color and black and white. This volume goes hand-in-hand with his book, *The Complete Photographer*. Reading this book will be time well spent.

Your Programs from Kodak. Kodak Publication No. T 1, Audio Visual Service, Eastman Kodak Company, Rochester, New York, 14650.

A catalogue of over 40 free programs on film and slides that can be borrowed from the Eastman Kodak Company. Includes programs on travel, how to take pictures, cameras, film, photography in education and so forth. Good material for faculty or club meetings. Order this 52-page booklet free of charge from the address above.

MAGAZINES

US Camera and Travel

Issued monthly at $5.00 per year. Excellent all-around magazine which contains an article on travel and the camera each month as well as book reviews, question and answer columns and articles of general photographic interest.

Subscription address: P.O. Box 562
                             Des Moines, Iowa 50302

II. Travel Magazines

Below is a representative but not exhaustive listing of travel magazines that are useful in researching the target areas, identifying places of interest for a trip and locating addresses for information.

Although subscription addresses are furnished, it is suggested that you look before you buy.

HOLIDAY

Subscription address: Box 1988
                             Independence Square
                             Philadelphia, Pa. 19105

NATIONAL GEOGRAPHIC

Send dues to: The Secretary
                     National Geographic Society
                     Washington, D.C. 20036

SUNSET

Issued monthly. An excellent magazine for trip ideas both in the US and abroad.

Subscription address: Sunset Magazine
                             Menlo Park, California 94025

TRAVEL HORIZONS

It is a must for the die-hard traveler. Contains extensive listings of travel guides that may be purchased from the subscription address if not found locally, index of travel films, tour operators, cruises, tours, etc. Excellent source for those planning to take organized tours. The magazine is designed as a liaison between the traveler and a professional travel agent.

Subscription address:　Travel Horizons
　　　　　　　　　　　　Ingledue Travel Publications
　　　　　　　　　　　　5850 Hollywood Blvd.
　　　　　　　　　　　　Hollywood, California 90028

III. Travel Guides for Travel Abroad

Your mode of travel and interests have a great bearing upon your choice of travel guides. This list provides a few to begin your planning. Several good guides are published in Europe in several languages and are not on this list. Of those, two popular ones are Turopa and Shell. Obtain a guide that discusses various motor routes and the sights one can expect to see on these routes. You would not need that type if flying from city to city or traveling by train.

Fodor's Modern Guides
This is the personal choice of the writer when in Europe. Fodor produces guides for the countries of Western Europe and Yugoslavia in separate volumes for each country or group of countries such as Benelux, Scandinavia, etc. His guide to the Caribbean, Bahamas and Bermuda is in one volume. Fodor also has a *Man's Guide to Europe, Woman's Guide to Europe* and *Jet Age Guide to Europe*. His guidebooks are in excellent format and are very comprehensive.

New Horizons: World Guide
Pan American's travel facts about 108 countries with thumbnail sketches by Gerald W. Whitted. Address inquiries or comments to: Pan American World Airways, P.O. Box PAA, Idlewild, N.Y.

Olsen, Harvey S. *Aboard and Abroad.* Subtitle, *Complete Travel Guide to Europe.* Philadelphia: J. B. Lippincott Co. About $6.95
Travel experts seem to like this particular book. Be sure to get a current issue if you buy one.

IV. Travel Guides for the United States

American Automobile Association
The AAA has an excellent and extensive travel service for members. Guides, maps and sightseeing information are provided free of charge. International travel service is also available to include the ordering of automobiles for foreign delivery. All travelers should investigate the benefits of AAA membership. If there is not an office in your locale, write for information to:
　　　　　　　　　　　　American Automobile Association
　　　　　　　　　　　　1712 G Street, N.W.
　　　　　　　　　　　　Washington, D.C.

USEFUL ADDRESSES

Maps and information about these countries, including their camping facilities, may be obtained from:

Austria
Austrian State Tourist Bureau
444 Madison Avenue
New York, N.Y. 10022

Belgium
Belgian Tourist Bureau
589 Fifth Avenue
New York, N.Y. 10017

Britain
British Travel Association
680 Fifth Avenue
New York, N.Y. 10020

France
French Government Tourist Office
610 Fifth Avenue
New York, N.Y. 10036

Canada
Also Yukon and Northwest Territories
Canadian Government Travel Bureau
Ottawa, Ontario

Canadian Provinces
Alberta Travel Bureau
Legislative Building
Edmonton, Alberta

British Columbia
Government Travel Bureau
Victoria, B.C.

Manitoba Bureau of Travel &
Publicity
Winnipeg, Manitoba

New Brunswick Travel Bureau
Fredericton, N.B.

Germany
German Tourist Information Office
500 Fifth Avenue
New York, N.Y. 10036

Italy
Italian State Tourist Office
626 Fifth Avenue
New York, N.Y. 10020

Sweden
Swedish National Travel Office
630 Fifth Avenue
New York, N.Y. 10020

Switzerland
Swiss National Tourist Office
10 West 49th Street
New York, N.Y. 10020

Newfoundland Tourist Development
Office
St. John's, Newfoundland

Nova Scotia Bureau of Information
Halifax, Nova Scotia

Ontario Dept. of Travel & Publicity
67 College Street
Toronto, Ontario

Prince Edward Island Travel Bureau
Charlottestown,
Prince Edward Island

Quebec Tourist Bureau
Quebec City,
Quebec

Saskatchewan Tourist Branch
Legislative Building
Regina,
Saskatchewan

Foreign Tourist Offices

The addresses given will not be repeated as those offices are not limited to camping information.

Africa
    East Africa Tourist Travel Assoc.
    750 Third Avenue
    New York, N.Y. 10017
    South African Tourist Corp.
    610 Fifth Avenue
    New York, N.Y. 10020

Alaska
    Alaska Travel Division
    Juneau, Alaska 99801

Arab States
    Arab States Tourist Office
    120 East 56th Street
    New York, N.Y. 10022

Australia
    Australian National Travel Assoc.
    636 Fifth Avenue
    New York, N.Y. 10022

Brazil
    Brazilian Government Trade
        Bureau
    551 Fifth Avenue
    New York, N.Y. 10017

Canada
    Canadian Government Travel
        Bureau
    680 Fifth Avenue
    New York, N.Y. 10022

Caribbean
    Caribbean Tourist Assoc.
    20 East 46th Street
    New York, N.Y. 10017

Ceylon
    Ceylon Tourist Publicity Office
    P.O. Box 2748
    Grand Central Station
    New York, N.Y. 10017

Columbia
    Columbia National Tourist Board
    608 Fifth Avenue
    New York, N.Y. 10022

Czechoslovakia
    Tour Information:
        CEDOK Travel Bureau
        10 East 40th Street
        New York, N.Y. 10016

    General Information:
        Made-in Publicity-CR
        Opletalova 5
        Prague, Czechoslovakia

Denmark
    Danish National Travel Office
    588 Fifth Avenue
    New York, N.Y. 10036

Ecuador
    Ecuadorean-American Chamber of
        Commerce, Inc.
    15 Whitehall Street
    New York, N.Y. 10004

Finland
    Finnish National Travel Office
    10 East 40th Street
    New York, N.Y. 10016

Greece
    National Tourist Organization
        of Greece
    601 Fifth Avenue
    New York, N.Y. 10017

Guatemala
    Guatemala Tourist Office
    331 Madison Avenue
    New York, N.Y. 10017

Haiti
    Haiti Government Tourist Bureau
    30 Rockefeller Plaza
    New York, N.Y. 10020

Hawaii
    Hawaii Visitors Bureau
    2270 Kalakaua Avenue
    Honolulu, Hawaii 96815

Hong Kong
Hong Kong Travel Association
501 Madison Avenue
New York, N.Y. 10022
or
291 Geary Street
San Francisco, California 94102

Iceland
Icelandic Consulate General
551 Fifth Avenue
New York, N.Y. 10017

India
Government of India Office
19 East 49th Street
New York, N.Y. 10017

Ireland
Irish Tourist Office
33 East 50th Street
New York, N.Y. 10022

Israel
Israel Government Tourist Office
574 Fifth Avenue
New York, N.Y. 10036

Japan
Japan National Tourist Assoc.
45 Rockefeller Plaza
New York, N.Y. 10020

Luxembourg
Luxembourg Consulate General
200 East 42nd Street
New York, N.Y. 10016

Mexico
Mexico Information Office
677 Fifth Avenue
New York, N.Y. 10022

Monaco
Monaco Information Center
610 Fifth Avenue
New York, N.Y. 10018

Netherlands
Netherlands National Tourist Office
605 Fifth Avenue
New York, N.Y. 10018

New Zealand
New Zealand Travel Commissioner
630 Fifth Avenue
New York, N.Y. 10020

Norway
Norwegian National Office
290 Madison Avenue
New York, N.Y. 10017

Pacific Area
Pacific Area Travel Association
228 Grant Avenue
San Francisco, Calif. 94108

Philippines
Philippines Travel Office
535 Fifth Avenue
New York, N.Y. 10017

Poland
Polish-American Information Bureau
55 West 42nd Street
New York, N.Y. 10036

Portugal
Casa de Portugal
447 Madison Avenue
New York, N.Y. 10022

Spain
Spanish National Tourist Office
589 Fifth Avenue
New York, N.Y. 10017

Tahiti
Tahiti Tourist Bureau
323 Geary Street
San Francisco, Calif. 94102

Turkey
Turkish Information Office
500 Fifth Avenue
New York, N.Y. 10017

Venezuela
Venezuela Chamber of Commerce
of the US
233 Broadway
New York, N.Y. 10007

Yugoslavia
Yugoslav State Tourist Office
509 Madison Avenue
New York, N.Y. 10022

17

Exploring the Global Village: The Human Heart of Social Studies

Myra B. Cook

> *Our new environment compels commitment and participation. We have become irrevocably involved with, and responsible for, each other.*
>
> Marshall McLuhan

ABOUT THE AUTHOR

Myra Cook attended Rollins College, the University of Florida and Cornell University. She graduated from Florida with a Bachelor of Arts in English and from Cornell with the Master of Education degree. Mrs. Cook has taught multiple and single grades in Florida and in Germany with the U. S. Army Dependents Schools. She was associated with the Homebound Teaching Program of Lawton, Oklahoma and the Army Education Center at Ft. Sill, Oklahoma. She conducted reading improvement courses for military personnel at both Ft. Sill and Ft. Chaffee, Arkansas. She is the author of the book *Chalkdust* and co-author of *The Come-Alive Classroom*.

The study of the globe—its peoples, geography, history and cultures—this is the business of social studies. In the elementary school the textbook travelog is gay and exciting, the costumes pretty, the festivals fun. But the child who will read it has been raised with TV. He has already looked far beyond the story presentations of rice paddies, alpine pastures and the steppe.

"The medium of our time—electric technology—is reshaping and restructuring patterns of social interdependence and every aspect of our personal life."* The enormity of the world's problems is staggering—but children are no longer sheltered from the knowledge of these problems. They have seen assassinations, picket lines, rioters. The unit on Community Helpers—firemen and police—has been dramatically enacted on the evening news. War, poverty, disease, trouble spill over the television screens into their living rooms and their lives. In comparison, the social studies text must seem a pleasant piece of fiction. They see Africa, Asia, Europe, North and South America through the close-up lens and they know there are many truths to be learned about their world that do not appear in social studies texts. This is not to despair. This is to acknowledge that there are vital social studies topics which must be faced with concern and resolve—children see them on TV, they see them in the community and in the neighborhood. They come to school for answers.

Thus, social studies becomes more than exports and imports, leading products, outstanding geographical features, festivals and costumes. Social studies is Life on This Globe, the teacher can say—and here's to a better one for all of us!

    ✔ What's being done?
    ✔ Who's doing it?
    ✔ What can we do?

Youngsters *can* make a personal response to the awesome task of building a better world for all humanity. It *is* possible to help. Learning that there are problems is the first step, relating them to their own lives is the second, and wanting to solve them, the third. Even the most modest investment of time, talent and or money can say, "I care." By doing whatever they can to insure that present and future generations have a chance at healthy, productive lives, children have guaranteed a brighter tomorrow for themselves. These are not platitudes. Today's world is a global village, says Marshall McLuhan. "Our new environment compels commitment and participation. We have become irrevocably involved with, and responsible for, each other."

There are many, many ways to explore this global village:

■ The social studies text can be supplemented by bulletins, advertisements, newspaper and magazine articles, non-fiction books, television specials and personal interviews.

*Marshall McLuhan and Quentin Fiore, *The Medium Is the Message*. New York: Bantam Books, 1967.

© Project Concern, Inc.

© Project Concern, Inc.

There are hundreds of worthy non-profit organizations deserving of interest and assistance around the world. They will gladly send bulletins describing the scope of their work and explaining the problems they are trying to solve.

American-Korean Foundation, Inc. The American-Korean Foundation provides thousands of scholarships for youngsters in Korea where all students pay tuition after the sixth grade.

- Take one of their children. Build a bulletin board around his case history. Ask your students to compare his life and country to their own, to look at his needs and to think about the ways they might be met. Use the textbook and the encyclopedia but turn also to the agencies at work with the people in this area or country.

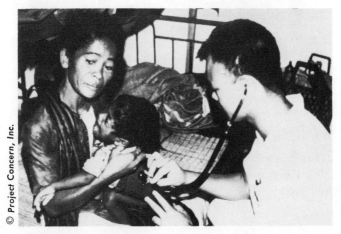

© Project Concern, Inc.

■ Pen-pals in another part of the state, the United States or abroad are wonderful contacts. Correspond with a whole classroom. Write to teachers in the Dependents Schools overseas. Choose any town in the USA, address a letter to the grade level teacher in the elemntary school there and propose your plan. Exchange thoughts, work, projects, souvenirs, snapshots, photography—any means by which another area of the world can be brought into sharp focus in your classroom.

■ Missionhurst sponsors a program—*Operation Happy Child*—in which a child's education is guaranteed for a semester by the pledge of a small sum. The sponsors receive the youngster's picture and his report cards throughout the year. They are invited to write to him, send small gifts such as ball point pens, erasers and the like, to become a personal friend. Jeng Dung Yang and Yang Su Jen are two such children. They and their classmates have made Taipai, Taiwan a very real and exciting spot on the globe to their American friends.

Americans sponsor the education of Jeng Dung Yang and Yang Su Yen of Taiwan and receive their report cards throughout the year.

■ Children can identify with men and women who have accepted
the responsibilities of world citizenship.
- They can learn about the doctors and nurses on the
  hospital ship HOPE and in MEDICO and PROJECT
  CONCERN who take working vacations, giving their
  time and talent to human beings in desperate need.

© Project Concern, Inc.

Children can learn about men and women who take working vacations, giving their time and talent to human beings
in desperate need.

- They can be told about the teenagers at Olinville
  Junior High School in the Bronx who voted through
  their student council to help a Vietnamese child and
  family. "The aim is not merely to buy a child a warm
  coat, a few meals and a new pair of shoes. Instead—
  funds are used to give a child, his family and a village
  a chance to permanently increase their income. And
  hopefully, permanently end their need for charity."

These are social studies that matter. These are solutions that children
should know about.

■ *Reader's Digest* published the account of American foster parents meeting their "son" in Greece for the first time seven years
after adoption. They had supported this young man through high
school and into college. Now he would tell them in person what it
had meant. "I will not thank you because I cannot. I can only pray
to God that someday, somehow, I will help someone as you have
helped me." The world, a global village, with each of us becoming
aware, learning to care, wanting to share.

The elementary teacher spends the day preparing children for responsible citizenship. Compassion, concern, involvement—these are social

These Bronx teenagers have found a peaceful way to fight in Vietnam. But they need your help.

Jones Wong, Janet Crawford and Robert Cirkiel are three of the leaders. But there are 2400 more like them at Olinville Junior High School in the Bronx. The youngest is 12. The oldest, 15. All of them are helping a Vietnamese child and his family in their fight against hunger and despair.

Last year, the student council at Olinville voted to share some of its good fortune with a Vietnamese child and family struggling to survive in a refugee camp. Through *Save The Children Federation* they're giving $15 a month to help the Nguyen Huans—a family of five with two sons, eight and four, and a daughter six.

The Huans lost everything in the war and for two years have been sharing a tiny room with another family. There is no privacy, no electricity, no running water, and one daily loaf of bread between them. The father works as a laborer for 50¢ a day. The mother spends her day collecting firewood for cooking and heat. And the eight-year-old son takes care of the two little ones.

The $15 each month provided by the children from Olinville Junior High has already had startling effects. It is providing the Huans with desperately needed clothes and food. With a small loan, the father has been able to start a small store in the family's half room. The money left over, together with money provided by other American sponsors, was borrowed by the refugee camp to help build a community market place and, most important, a school. The Huans are still a long way from winning the battles against hunger and poverty. But despair is giving way to hope.

Peace may one day come to Vietnam. But for hundreds of thousands the eventual solution won't help unless they get food and clothes right now, and a reason to believe that the future will be brighter. Your help is needed to give them a little

boost to help them to begin helping themselves.

That's what *Save The Children* is all about. Although your contribution of $15 a month is tax-deductible, it's not charity. The aim is not merely to buy a child a warm coat, a few meals and a new pair of shoes. Instead your funds are used to give a child, his family and a village a chance to permanently increase their income. And hopefully, permanently end their need for charity.

As a sponsor you can select a Vietnamese child. Or a child in Korea, Latin America, Africa, or Greece. You will receive a photo of the child, regular reports on his progress, and if you wish, a chance to correspond with the child and his family. Teenagers from the Bronx are doing it. Can you, your family, or your group do the same?

We won't promise you that your $15 a month is going to save the world. Just a small

piece of it. But, maybe that is the way to save the world, if there are enough of you out there.

Save The Children Federation is registered with the U.S. State Department Advisory Committee on Voluntary Foreign Aid. Financial statements and annual reports are available upon request.

National Sponsors (partial list): Faith Baldwin, Mrs. James Bryant Conant, Joan Crawford, Hon. James A. Farley, Jerry Lewis, Henry R. Luce, Frank Sinatra, Mrs. Earl Warren.

Save The Children Federation
NORWALK, CONNECTICUT 06852

I WISH TO CONTRIBUTE $180 ANNUALLY TO HELP A CHILD IN
☐ KOREA ☐ GREECE ☐ VIETNAM ☐ LATIN AMERICA ☐ AFRICA
☐ WHERE THE NEED IS GREATEST.
ENCLOSED IS MY FIRST PAYMENT
☐ $15.00 MONTHLY   ☐ $45.00 QUARTERLY
☐ $90.00 SEMI-ANNUALLY   ☐ $180.00 ANNUALLY
I CAN'T SPONSOR A CHILD. ENCLOSED IS A CONTRIBUTION OF
$_____ ☐ PLEASE SEND ME MORE INFORMATION.
NAME _____
ADDRESS _____
CITY _____ STATE _____ ZIP _____
CONTRIBUTIONS ARE INCOME TAX DEDUCTIBLE   NY 1/14/7

© *Save the Children Federation.*

studies words which can be brought to life in the child's vocabulary. If people around the world are real to the children in your class—if their existence, their personalities, their needs and problems are felt to be as important as their own, if they want for others all the good things they wish for themselves, then the purpose of social studies will have been achieved.

© Care, Inc.

The world, a global village, with each of us becoming
aware, learning to care, wanting to share.

• Here are just a few of the many worthy organizations which can help children learn about their neighbors around the globe:

Project Concern, Inc.
P.O. Box 2468
San Diego, Calif. 92112

Save the Children Federation
49 Boston Road
Norwalk, Conn. 06852

Care
660 First Ave.
New York, N.Y. 10016

St. Labre Indian School
Ashland,
Montana 59003

Korean Relief, Inc.
P.O. Box 6121
Washington, D.C. 20044

Missionhurst
4651 N. 25th St.
Arlington, Va. 22207

Foster Parents Plan, Inc.
352 Park Avenue, So.
New York, N.Y. 10010

Compassion
7774 Irving Park Rd.
Chicago, Ill. 60634

UNICEF
United Nations
New York, N.Y. 10017

VISTA
Washington, D.C. 20506

Peace Corps
Washington, D.C. 20525

American-Korean Foundation
345 E. 46th St.
New York, N.Y. 10017

Thomas A. Dooley Foundation
442 Post St.
San Francisco, Calif. 94102

Good Ship HOPE
2233 Wisconsin Ave., NW
Washington, D.C. 20007

Pallottine Missions
309 N. Paca St.
Baltimore, Md. 21201

Salesian Missions
2 Lefevre Lane
New Rochelle, N.Y. 10802

• Reading material to help with global understanding:

Pearl Buck
CHILDREN FOR ADOPTION
New York: Random House, 1957

Georges Carousso
"THE DAY WE MET OUR SON"
Reader's Digest, March 1968

Thomas A. Dooley, M.D.
DELIVER US FROM EVIL
New York: Farrar, Straus, 1956

EDGE OF TOMORROW
New York: Farrar, Straus, 1958

THE NIGHT THEY BURNED THE MOUNTAIN
New York: Farrar, Straus, 1960

Albert Schweitzer
OUT OF MY LIFE AND THOUGHT
New York: Holt, 1949

James A. Turpin, M.D.
VIETNAM DOCTOR
New York: McGraw-Hill, 1967

"THE REVOLUTION OF RISING EXPECTATIONS"
San Diego: Project Concern, Inc., 1967

18

Television and the Classroom Teacher

Eva Baldwin Jones

ABOUT THE AUTHOR

Eva Jones received her BS degree from Cheyney State College in Cheyney, Pennsylvania. She has taught in the elementary schools of Philadelphia and Baltimore and was a television teacher for the Baltimore City Schools. Mrs. Jones has conducted several experimental programs: the Language Experience Approach to Reading, the Non-Graded Primary and the Cuisenaire—Gattengo System of Teaching Mathematics. She prepared and taught a series of social studies lessons on WJZ-TV, Baltimore and a series of geometry lessons on WBAL-TV, Baltimore.

Education "Discovers" Television

The organization of learning experiences is more difficult than a few decades ago. Not only are there more students to teach, but there is more information to be taught. Advances such as classroom TV can help solve some of these problems. Through television your students can travel around the globe while sitting in the classroom. Each student has a ringside seat as events unfold before his eyes. No longer is bodily attendance at art museums, musical programs, and dramatic performances necessary. Television is a powerful and dynamic tool. If used wisely, it can help you do a more effective job.

This chapter concerns itself with the practical information necessary to appreciate and make better use of television in the classroom.

What Is Instructional Television?

Educational television means many things to many people, because almost all television programs have some educational value. Instructional television is more specific, in that it is designed for direct use in the classroom. It usually means a fully equipped studio, a television teacher, and students viewing the telecast in many scattered classrooms. Televised instruction may originate from a commercial or educational TV station, or be transmitted by closed circuit.

Present Uses

In general there are four primary uses of instructional television in education.

1. DIRECT TEACHING BY TELEVISION:
   The major portion of a course is presented by the studio teacher.
   Example: Foreign languages
2. AS A SUPPLEMENTARY TEACHING AID:
   Televised instruction assumes part of the teaching load, but the major portion of instruction remains with the classroom teacher.
   Example: Social studies
3. TELEVISION AS ENRICHMENT:
   The viewing of special events and programs, while not directly related to any particular course, has educational value.
   Example: Inauguration of public officials, space flights, etc.
4. TELEVISION AS TOTAL TEACHING:
   Where an entire course is taught without assistance of the classroom teacher.
   Example: Complete college courses such as "Continental Classroom."

A Look at Research

Although it's too early to draw any final conclusions about television's role in education, current research has been encouraging. These results show in some cases that students learn about as much, and sometimes more than by conventional methods. However, in most cases, there has been no significant difference in achievement. These findings are better appreciated when one considers the newness of instructional television, the lack of experience, and improper facilities. There are two prime reasons for instructional television's limited success; the quality of programs and their use in the classroom. Many more teachers need to become familiar with the skills of teaching on and with television.

Advantages of Television

1. Television can make use of all other audio-visual materials without losing the one-to-one relationship.
2. As a teaching tool television can magnify tiny objects for many to see at the same time with equal visual advantages.
3. It reduces large or distant objects not normally available for classroom use.
4. Television can be viewed simultaneously by a large number of students in different locations.
5. It can extend the well prepared presentation of a gifted teacher.
6. Television has proven to be an excellent motivational tool.
7. Television has a tremendous range of possible uses. It can provide supplementary materials, or be the foundation for an entire course.

Both Sides of the Picture Tube

Just as the studio teacher has had classroom experience, it is important for the classroom teacher to have some knowledge of what a TV teacher does, and what goes into the preparation of a lesson. The following section is designed to bring about this kind of mutual understanding.

The Television Teacher

The classroom and TV teacher form a team, each depending upon the other for help. In addition, the TV teacher must be able to adjust her

The TV teacher can reach a large number of students in different locations simultaneously. (WBAL-TV Photo)

teaching to the limitations of television and at the same time make full use of its advantages. She must have enough confidence to teach in front of cameras and crew, to feel an audience that cannot be seen, to stimulate interaction and anticipate questions. These ingredients help to develop a rapport between TV teachers and viewers.

The Classroom Teacher

It is the classroom teacher who prepares the students for the TV programs. She clarifies points, answers questions, leads discussions, and gives individual help. It is the classroom teacher who decides what she expects her children to get out of the lessons. The final success of any television program greatly depends upon the teacher's attitude.

Selecting the Program

After the classroom teacher has been made aware of the TV offerings in her school, she must then determine which of these programs can be used. The following guidelines will be helpful when selecting TV programs.

1. The program should fit comfortably into the class schedule.
2. The teacher should know exactly what objectives she wants the telecast to cover.
3. The telecast material should fall within the interest range and attention span of the children.
4. The materials and equipment to carry out the lesson should be readily accessible.

After choosing a program the teacher can proceed with plans for its use.

Preparing Students for Television

The amount of preparation for a lesson depends largely upon the type of program and how it is to be used. However, it is important for the teacher to give the students any background information necessary and in keeping with the purpose of the lesson.

The following activities are suggested:

1. Summarize what students already know about the topic.
2. Attempt to carry out the suggestions in the teachers' guide.
3. List key questions about the topic on the blackboard.
4. Make bulletin board displays concerning the topic.
5. Conduct activities that develop good listening and viewing habits.

6. Make reading material available on the topic.
7. Familiarize children with any necessary vocabulary.
8. Encourge children to bring to class as many related materials as possible.
9. Discuss ways of finding out about the world around us.
10. Tell or read a story or poem in connection with the topic.
11. Help children recall visits to places related to the topic.
12. Take children on a tour stressing words, etc.
13. Locate and trace related places on a large wall map.
14. Discuss various methods of obtaining information.
15. Develop technique of interviewing, practice through role playing.

Organizing the Classroom

Some of the physical features with which the teacher must be concerned are:

TV SETS

1. The TV sets should be raised high enough for comfortable viewing.
2. Check picture quality before telecast.

ROOM LIGHTING

1. The room should not be darkened.
2. The set should be placed away from windows to reduce glare.
3. Place the set so that no student is looking directly into the light.

SEATING

1. The screen size determines the seating arrangement for proper viewing.
2. Care should be taken to place students with poor vision in the more advantageous seats.
3. The difference in student heights should be taken into account.

During the Telecast

The classroom teacher should do whatever is necessary to see to it that her children get the most out of the telecasts. While there is no definite procedure to follow the teacher should:

1. Actively respond to the lesson.

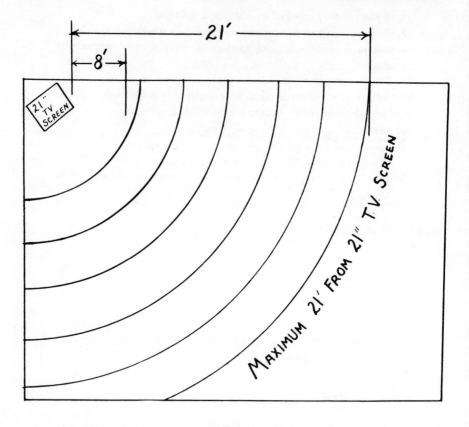

2. Record items to be clarified.
3. Recognize children who need additional help.
4. Encourage children to respond to directions and questions.

Follow-up Activities

The teacher should use a variety of activities to follow-up a lesson. Whether dealing with total groups, small groups, or individuals, each activity should have a definite purpose which expands the TV program.

The following is a sampling of various types of follow-up activities:

SCIENCE

- Experiments based on program
- Collecting specimens
- Report on famous scientists
- Set up science corner
- Science notebooks

- Discuss and list ways to answer questions in science
- Find out about the tools and methods of scientific inquiry
- Make use of science books, films and filmstrips
- Make use of local resources, people, places and things.

WRITING

- Stories, poems, letters
- Taking notes, making reports, outlines
- Articles for school paper
- List vocabulary words
- Making labels and titles for exhibits
- Making a list of books related to the TV series.

READING

- Examine books in the classroom
- Visit school library
- Visit public library
- Magazine and newspapers
- Teacher-prepared materials
- Charts and graphs

MUSIC

- Listening to records
- Listening to special broadcasts
- Group singing
- Instrumental presentations
- Explaining how instruments work
- Making tapes
- Rhythm bands
- Making instruments such as Maracas, drums, rattles
- Interpreting and dramatizing music spontaneously
- Finding information for bulletin board displays about music and musicians.

ART

- Scrapbooks
- Sculpturing
- Displays
- Drawings and paintings
- Models and mobiles
- Puppets and puzzles

- Collages
- Murals
- Hand movies

- Making maps and charts
- Bulletin board and table displays
- Diagrams

The Cooperative Approach

The success of any instructional television program depends upon two teachers; the studio teacher, and the classroom teacher. Both teachers are interested in the subject, the students, and teaching. The combined skills of these two teachers can bring about far more effective teaching than either one could achieve alone. This cooperative approach is of utmost importance even though the two teachers are in different locations.

Sample Evaluation Sheet

Where studio and classroom teacher cannot meet with one another, it is helpful to provide feedback from the classroom to studio. The following is a sample check sheet which can be used by the classroom teacher to help the studio teacher evaluate the telecasts.

BALTIMORE CITY PUBLIC SCHOOLS

Radio-TV-Department

School_____ Principal_____

Classroom Teacher_____ Grade_____

Subject_____ Date_____

Number of students viewing_____

EVALUATION OF PRIMARY "MODERN MATH" SERIES

1. Were the topics discussed timely ones?   Yes___ No___
2. Were the topics fully developed?   Yes___ No___
3. Was there too much emphasis on language?   Yes___ No___
4. Were the lessons visually effective?   Yes___ No___
5. Were the lessons
        too long_____ too short_____ just right_____?
6. Were the children interested?   Yes___ No___
7. Did the lessons help you?   Yes___ No___
8. Were the lessons arranged so that you could use
   them as introductory lessons_____ review lessons_____ or
   culminating lessons?_____

9. What topics would you like to see next year?_____

10. COMMENTS: _____

Other Sources of Information

When you begin making use of television you will want to find out as much about it as you can. You will want to know what the schools have done with it, and how it has developed. The following suggestions are ways in which you can get additional information.

WORKSHOPS

Workshops and even college seminars are being widely used to serve as a sounding board for constructive discussion, and to share one another's experiences concerning television. These workshops and seminars are proving to be very helpful in learning new methods and techniques for teaching with TV.

OBSERVING OTHER CLASSES

There are few teachers, no matter how experienced, who cannot learn from others. Observing another class during a telecast can also be helpful in learning good techniques and procedures. When you try using these techniques in your classroom, you will have a chance to be creative and develop new methods of your own.

VISITING THE STUDIO

Whenever possible, you should visit the television teacher in the studio to observe a telecast being presented. Only then can you really appreciate the work, time, and pressures that go into each lesson.

Color adds another dimension to televised instruction. (WJZ-TV Photo)

Television can make use of other audio-visual materials. Film projector (left), and slide chain (right). (WJZ-TV Photo)

This color videotape machine makes it possible to save programs for future use. (WJZ-TV Photo)

WJZ-TV Eyewitness News Set. (WJZ-TV Photo)

READING

Although ITV is still relatively young, it has amassed quite a bibliography. Many books, pamphlets, research papers, and articles have been written on this subject. Certainly a complete listing of all the reading

Studio Control Room.

TV Director at Switcher. (WJZ-
TV Photo)

Master Control Room. (WJZ-
TV Photo)

material available would be impossible at this time. However, here is a
sampling of some up-to-date material which is available.

National Education Association, *And TV Too!*, National Education
Association, Washington, D.C.   1961   63p.
Stanford University Institute for Communication Research, *The
Next Ten Years*, Educational Television, Institute for Communi-
cation Research, Stanford University, Stanford, California   1962

Costello, Lawrence F., & Gordon, George N., *Teach with Television: A Guide to Instructional Television*, Hastings House, New York, N.Y.   1961

Smith, Mary Howard, Ed. *Using Television in the Classroom*, McGraw-Hill, New York, N.Y.   1961

Public and Private Agencies

Unfortunately, there is no one centralized place where you can get all of the desired information about ITV. Nevertheless, there are a number of public and private agencies that can be very helpful simply by having your name placed on their mailing lists.

> Division of Audio-Visual Instructional Service
> National Education Association
> 1201 Sixteenth Street, N.W.
> Washington, D.C.

> Ford Foundation and Fund for the Advancement of Education
> 477 Madison Ave.
> New York, N.Y.

> National Association of Educational Broadcasters (NAEB)
> Coliseum Building
> 10 Columbus Circle
> New York, N.Y.

> Radio-Television Office
> U.S. Office of Education
> Washington, D.C.

Instructional Television and Teaching—
Partners in Progress

If students are to learn more and faster, Instructional TV and teaching must move ahead hand in hand. Television is one of the most significant educational tools of the present and the immediate future. It's a way of reaching and teaching today's children more effectively. Proper use of instructional television will eventually up-date teaching. Progressive teaching can explore the full contribution of television.

The final success of instructional television depends upon what hundreds and thousands of classroom teachers do in the next few years. Will it help your students? It's up to you!

19

Be Three Places at Once in an Audio-Visual Classroom

Dale S. Devine

ABOUT THE AUTHOR

Dale Devine received her Bachelor of Arts Degree in English from Carleton College and the Master of Education degree from Cornell University. She has taught second and third graders in the Irondequoit Schools of Rochester, New York, in Kaiserslautern, Germany with the U. S. Army Dependent Schools and in the Hinsdale, Illinois School System. She contributed material to *The Come-Alive Classroom* and co-authored *"From Crib to Kindergarten, A Primer for Parents"* which won first prize in *Scholastic Teacher's* 1968 Promising New Practices in Elementary Education Contest. Mrs. Devine has given PTA programs and conducted teacher workshops on the use of audio-visual equipment in the classroom.

Would you like to be in two places at once? or three? or four? It can be done, thanks to the magic of modern teaching materials! Look over your class. Decide

- who needs special help,
- who is ready for enrichment,
- which concepts need clearing up,
- which subjects require extra drill.

Now look over your school's supply of audio-visual equipment. Make plans to use it *effectively*! Much equipment sits, just waiting for someone to discover it.

■ Take time out to get acquainted with each machine. Learn all its capabilities:

    ✔ read the manual,

    ✔ practice in private,

    ✔ watch a teacher who uses it regularly,

    ✔ ask the company representative to give a demonstration.

Introducing the machine to your class is all important. Build it up! Make it special! If children think it is a privilege to use the machine, they'll beg for a turn. If they think they *have* to use it, they'll quickly lose interest. Be sure children know the proper use of each machine: which buttons can be pushed and which are "hands off." (For young children, use colored tape to label switches or buttons—red for DO NOT TOUCH, blue for TOUCH.)

Often children who are academically poor are mechanically able. Capitalize on this! Let these children be in charge of the audio-visual equipment They'll gain self-esteem and the respect of the class. And repeated viewing or listening to educational material is bound to have some effect!

MOVIES

Movies are one of the oldest and most familiar of the audio-visual aids. Are you using the projector in your building to its best advantage? Movies are invaluable in all areas of the curriculum.

How else, but through the "miracle" of time-lapse photography, can you watch a morning glory burst into blossom or a bean send down roots? Most elementary classrooms are set up only for the most simple of experiments. Choose films which present experiments. Every child gets a front row seat.

Field trips are wonderful but no class can visit the many parts of the globe it studies. Movies can take you there. Movies can take you back in time or thrust you into the future. They can bring you the best from the world of the theater. They can put trained artists in your classroom, demonstrating techniques you could never teach.

> Keep a simple record from year to year of the movies which are best for each subject. Titles are similar but there can be a big difference between two films on the same subject!

Presenting the film properly can insure its success:

■ Discuss what you hope to see, what you want to learn.

■ Make a list of things to look for or questions to answer.

- Stop the projector whenever necessary.
  - Turn it off to ask a question.
  - If the class hasn't observed carefully, reverse the film and play the section over.
- Ask questions! A social studies or science movie is being presented for subject matter. If children are expecting a stimulating class discussion, they'll pay close attention.
  - Even young children can take notes and use them as a basis for questioning their classmates.
  - Take notes yourself so you won't forget major points or small but interesting details.
- Don't stop with who? where? and what? questions. Encourage independent thought.
  - What did this movie show that couldn't be seen in a class?
  - Why did you like (or dislike) this film?
  - How was this movie made? (It takes some thought for primary students to realize a movie about Pilgrim times wasn't filmed in the 1600's. Let them try to figure out how it was made; or how shots of Indians hunting buffalo were taken).
  - If your school is in the market for a new projector, investigate the kind that has a stop action. With this feature you can stop the machine at a single frame and discuss the picture in detail.

Is setting up a projector and screen a bother? Consider getting a projection cart. The projector is set up and focused; the screen is part of the cart. Whenever you need it, wheel the cart into the room; thread the film and it's ready to go.

FILMSTRIP PROJECTOR

A filmstrip projector is "so easy even a child can operate it." Let them!
- Once the machine is threaded, any youngster in your room can become a filmstrip operator.
  - An easel or chalkboard, with white paper taped on, makes an effective screen. It's quick to set up and takes less space than an ordinary screen.
  - If only one or two children will be watching, use a filmstrip previewer. It fits right on the child's desk.
- Use filmstrips for enrichment.
  - *Some children are ready for more advanced math?* Let them learn about fractions from a filmstrip while you review number facts with the rest of the class.

- *One child shows a deeper interest in a subject than his classmates?* Set him aside with filmstrips to explore related areas of study.
- *Committees can work on reports studying geography, customs or people of other lands.* Be sure one member of each committee is capable of reading the narration, or provide filmstrips that come with records. Many new ones are listed in the catalog from:

  Society for Visual Education, Inc.
  1345 Diversey Parkway
  Chicago, Illinois   60614

■ Use filmstrips and record combinations in your Language Arts program. Weston Woods has a series of children's classics. *Mike Mulligan & Stone Soup* come alive on filmstrip and record. Coronet films offers Indian legends and the Just So stories. The class can have a fascinating and enriching story hour while you tutor the child who's been absent or give diagnostic tests to a new child.

- Weston Woods offers (free of charge) a beautiful catalog and a series of reprints describing the work in their studio. Ask for:

  Morton Schindel: Creator of "Picture Book Parade" by Ruth B. Walker (Reprinted from November 1962 Elem. English)

  There's Action in Stills by Harvey Fondiller (Reprinted from Popular Photography)

  Confessions of a Book Fiend by Morton Schindel. (Reprinted from Feb. 1967 School Library Journal)

  Curtain of Illusion—The Odyssey of the Children's Caravan by John Poignand and Peggy Mann (Reprinted from Feb. 1967 School Library Journal)

  To order, write:

  Weston Woods
  Weston, Conn.   06880

MICROSCOPE PROJECTOR

If your school needs a new filmstrip projector, buy one with a microscope slide attachment. Project your slide of snail eggs or plant cells on a screen. All the class will see the *same* image! You can point out and discuss parts of the slide. No more problems about not having enough microscopes to go around—and you know the children are seeing what you want them to see.

For information about all types of projectors, ear phones, films, filmstrips and transparencies, ask for the Education Catalog from:

> Central Scientific
> Cenco Center
> 2600 South Kostner Ave.
> Chicago, Illinois   60623

Write to Eye Gate for separate catalogs on filmstrips, records, cartridged Teach-A-Tapes, overhead transparencies, 16mm films, 8mm single concept film loops and related instructional charts and aids.

> Eye Gate House, Inc.
> 146–01 Archer Avenue
> Jamaica, New York   11435

FILMLOOP PROJECTOR

Single concept film loops have been on the educational scene for some time but they are just beginning to make their way into the elementary classroom. Most machines are so simple, a primary student, once instructed, can insert the cassette and start the film. Because they are continuous loops, there's never a need to rewind. Look through a-v catalogs and select the loops applicable to your course of study. They are *much* cheaper than movies. One film company offering primary level loops is

> Popular Science
> 355 Lexington Ave.
> New York, New York

Children love to watch film loops of growing plants or insect cycles. And with each viewing they seem to discover something new!

PHONOGRAPH

The phonograph is often standard but neglected equipment. With ear phones and a jack (which can easily be installed if your record player doesn't have one), children can be having a variety of directed activities while you are busy with reading groups or review.

■ Make sure record, speed, and needle match by using a color key.

- Put a spot of yellow tape on the label of all 33⅓ records. Put a matching spot of color by the 33⅓ speed control.
- Label 45 r.p.m. record and speed in green.
- Put spots of yellow and green on the l.p. needle.
- No color indicates 78 record, speed and needle.

■ Give frequent demonstrations on how to handle and care for records. Be on the safe side, though, and tape record each new record. It's cheaper than replacing scratched recordings!

Math Drill

Records provide marvelous math drills. Harcourt, Brace and World, Inc. has a series of Mathematics Skill Builders. Children listen to problems and write their responses in the proper spaces. Then they listen for the correct answers. The record provides background music while children study problems missed (listed by number on the back of the answer sheet). Then the record retests. Children are thrilled when they do better the second time. Other series give addition, subtraction, multiplication and division drill. The first records, or bands, have simple fact problems at spaced intervals. Children work up to more difficult problems worked at shorter intervals. Inquire about the "Six Wonderful Records of Facts" from

John D. Caddy

Box 251

Canoga Park, California

Write for information about "Math Made Meaningful" records from

Classroom Materials, Inc.

93 Myrtle Drive

Great Neck, New York

■ Musical multiplication records provide an interesting way of learning multiplication tables. Most children learn the lyrics to songs far more quickly than they do math facts. *Make sure the concept of multiplication has been taught first, then let children learn their facts in song.* The snappy rhythm is catchy and even you will soon be thinking "9 times 7 is 63" in time to music. You can find out more about "Musical Multiplication Records" from

Bremmer Records

Dept. S–7

Wilmette, Illinois   60091

■ Use math records for individual drill and help. Or use them with the entire class.

- Divide children into teams. Give a point to the first team to call out the right answer to the problem given on the record.
- Use math records for formal or informal testing. You are free to walk around the room, making notations:
  - ✔ *Which child still counts on his fingers?*
  - ✔ *Who is making marks on his desk?*
  - ✔ *Which children put down the answer immediately?*

Social Studies

Use records for enrichment in social studies. Songs from another land make the country come alive. Sounds of the city, seashore, or desert give children a "feeling" for the area being studied. Let children who finish work early listen to records—a good incentive for the slow workers! Write for a catalog from

> Folkways Scholastic Records
> 907 Sylvan Avenue
> Englewood Cliffs, New Jersey
> and
> Folkways Records, Inc.
> 117 W. 46th Street
> New York, N.Y.   10036

Science

Enrich your science program with Motivation Records' singing science series. Weather songs, Space songs, Nature and more Nature songs, Experiment, Energy and Motion songs all offer a wonderful way to learn new science concepts. Your class can be learning "why do leaves change their color?" while you are busy with someone who needs special attention. Or an advanced science pupil can learn the difference between "what is an animal, what is a plant?" while you are occupied with morning reading groups. Two catalogs listing these records, and many others, are published by:

> Valiant Instructional Materials Corporation
> 172 Walker Lane
> Englewood, New Jersey   07631
> and
> Enrichment Materials
> Education Visual Aids
> E. 64 Midland Avenue
> Paramus, New Jersey

Language Arts

Perk up your language arts program with Ginn and Company's "Imagi-Craft" series. The "Sounds and Images" records stimulate creative expression. Children are invited to listen to strange sounds, then to stretch their imaginations as they think what they might be.

Need help for the child who talks too much? Or for the shy new child? Play appropriate selections from "Teaching Children Values." Each unfinished story presents a common childhood situation. In trying to finish the story, your class may come up with solutions to the particular problem. And they'll all gain a better understanding of themselves and others. For information write:

> Education Activities, Inc.
> Freeport, Long Island
> New York

Reading

Are you looking for a sure-fire way to stimulate interest in independent reading? Bring book and record sets into the classroom.

- Scott Foresman's "First Talking Storybook Box" will give you attractive, hard-cover copies of the children's favorite books (republished with original text and illustrations). An unobtrusive "beep" on the record signals children when to turn the page as they follow the story.
- Look for Herr Wagner Publishing Company's series of Leonard books. In each book (beginning at a preprimer level) Leonard and his time machine explore some place of interest to a boy: dinosaur land, the ocean floor, outer space. The recorded voice goes very slowly, allowing even the poorest reader to keep up. While the pace is slow, the material is interesting enough to fascinate faster pupils. For information write to:

  > Herr Wagner Publishing Co.
  > 609 Mission St.
  > San Francisco, Calif.   94105

- Investigate Scholastic Book Club selections for very inexpensive book and record combinations. Paperback books and accompanying records are available for under a dollar. The story of Ferdinand is read with wonderful Spanish background and bullfight sound effects.

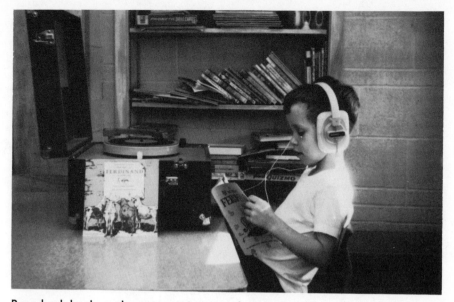

Paperback books and accompanying records are available
for under a dollar.

Vary the technique to fit the child. Some children will be more
stimulated to read if they can listen to the record first, while
looking at the book. Others should be "treated" to hearing the
record only after they've read the book on their own. If you
don't want young children handling the records, tape them.
Just be sure you label the tape carefully so you'll know where
each story selection begins.

- Have you used records to help with vowel sounds, final consonants, or blends? A whole reading group can listen together
or the single child who is having trouble can listen alone. Ask
to be included on the mailing list for:

Educational Record Sales
157 Chambers Street
New York, New York   10007

Look through your catalog collection carefully. You'll discover a wealth of recorded material just right for your class.

TAPE RECORDER

Buy pre-recorded tapes or make your own—but use that tape recorder!

Phonics

Make your own tapes to test sound recognition. Make ditto sheets for
blends or vowels.

You'll save time if you make dittos which can be used for several tapes. Ditto A can be used for either initial blends or endings. Ditto B can be used for initial or final consonants. Ditto C can be used for either long or short vowel sounds (or both, if children are to mark the vowel with ⏑ or —). Give all directions on the tape: "Listen carefully. Circle the vowel sound you hear. Number 1. *cat*. Do you hear a, e, i, o, or u? Circle the vowel you hear. CAT. Be sure to include a self-correcting session *at the end of the tape*. Repeat each word and give the answer. "Number 1. CAT. Short a. Did you mark a? Good!" Label your tapes well and store for repeated use.

Ditto A

1. ch sh th
2. th bl pr
3. ck ch th

Ditto B

1. d p b
2. s t h
3. m n t

Ditto C

1. a e i o u
2. a e i o u
3. a e i o u

Spelling

Give your spelling tests by tape recorder. Pre-record the tests. If you go through your spelling book you can do all the tests on a single tape and in a single taping session. Be sure to mark the footage where each test begins! Children will pay far closer attention to a tape, knowing it won't repeat or answer questions. You can move around the room noting how children work.

Use the tape to give make-up spelling tests to children who've been absent. Or make trial tests on another tape so children can practice during the week (just be sure the order is not the same as in the final test).

Creative Writing

Have a child who is creative but can't spell or write? Let him dictate stories into the tape recorder. Transcribe them later at your leisure. He'll be thrilled with the results and his creative instinct may be kept alive till his skills catch up.

Music

You can't play the piano? Ask the music teacher to tape the accompaniment to the class's songs.

Dramatics

You're giving a play? Record your practice.

For many new ideas and much practical advice, ask for a copy of "Creative Teaching with Tape" from:

> Revere-Mincom Division
> 3 M
> 2501 Hudson Road
> St. Paul, Minnesota   55119

LANGUAGE MASTER

Does your school system have a Bell and Howell Language Master? Speech and foreign language departments have put the Language Master to good use—but it is equally at home in the classroom. A concept, word or phrase is written or illustrated on the upper part of each Language Master card. The correct response is recorded on the magnetic tape at the bottom of the card. Children can record *their* response on the card, play it back, and see if it matches yours.

■ Children can use the Language Master in groups, with one child holding up the card, or they can use it alone. A word is read, the card put in the machine, then YOUR voice gives the correct response. If the child has said the word correctly, he puts it in the "right" pile. If not, he repeats until his answer matches yours. You may be on the other side of the room, but your pupil is corrected by your voice as soon as he makes a mistake.

Reading

Keep track of words missed in reading groups. Look ahead and jot down words likely to cause trouble. Record these words on Language Master cards. The assignment can be more specific: "Say the word, identify the vowel sound, give the rule." Or "Spell the picture word." Copy whole sentences from a primer for the slow reader.

Children can use the Language Master in groups, with one child holding up the card, or they can use it alone.

Vocabulary Enrichment

Enrich the vocabulary of quicker students.
- List new words to be read and defined.
- Make a set of cards for antonym practice. A card saying UP would call for the response DOWN. Or use the cards for syllabication drill.

Just make sure children understand what is expected each time you use the cards for a different assignment.

Arithmetic

Let the Language Master help with arithmetic. Write story problems on cards, record the solution. Draw pictures to illustrate problems. XXX XXX XXX to the beginning multiplication student calls for an answer of "3 groups of 3 is nine or 3 x 3 = 9." A simple math fact on a card which says the answer is far more exciting than a flash card which merely SHOWS the answer.

Social Studies

For social studies, outline states on Language Master cards. Have children identify and tell the capital of each. Use the cards for tree or bird identification: a picture on the card, the answer on the tape. Attach post cards of famous paintings. Let children learn to identify them by listening to the cards.

Language Master cards come in a variety of sizes. Big ones are best suited for pictures (how about color or number recognition for readiness work?). Small ones are more economical for single words. Bell and Howell sells pre-recorded sets (vocabulary builder, phonics program, beginning French). Blank cards can be tailored to fit your class's particular needs. If you know a certain word will be needed throughout the year write directly on the card with felt marker. However if it's a word or concept you'll need only briefly, write it on an index card. Staple or clip the word to the Language Master card. When you are through with it, remove it, make a new one, and retape. One set of cards can last indefinitely this way.

Use the Language Master for instant reinforcement! If a child is wrong, he corrects himself immediately. It can be almost as good as having a teacher for every pupil, and the pupil will probably think it more fun!

CONTROLLED READER

Have you seen a Controlled Reader? It is a filmstrip projector which presents stories, pictures, or mathematical problems at a controlled rate of speed. It can present material line by line or in a left to right progression. *Unlike most projectors, it can be used without darkening the room.* A group can work with the Controlled Reader without disturbing the rest of the class.

Not only does the Controlled Reader attempt to improve functional skills, but it offers a marvelous way to increase attention span and improve "sloppy" reading habits. Children quickly learn they must concentrate on the story as it unfolds. There's no looking back at the preceding page or paragraph for an answer. Some children who never seem to focus their complete attention on a page of printed matter, learn they must overlook classroom distractions if they are to understand the story. The filmstrip stories, sold in sets by grade level, are of high interest level. Lesson plans and student work books are available.

The Controlled Reader can be used to supplement the regular reading period. Once you have established the proper speed for the group, and have introduced the story and vocabulary, you need not be with the group. While the machine automatically reveals the story, you can observe *how* the children read, correct work, or give individual help elsewhere.

Vary your use of question sheets (either EDL prepared or teacher-made). Sometimes allow children to read the questions first before seeing

The Language Master can be used for instant reinforcement in many areas of the curriculum.

A group can work with the controlled reader without disturbing the rest of the class.

the filmstrip. At other times let them check their answers themselves as they read through the story a second time.

For more information about the Controlled Reader write to:

Educational Developmental Laboratories

284 E. Pulaski Road

Huntington, New York   11743

Inquire, too, about the company's revolutionary "Listen, Look, Learn" system for primary reading or its "Listen and Think" program for developing listening skills.

OVERHEAD PROJECTOR

The overhead projector is coming into its own in the elementary classroom. Because it spotlights the material, it's far more eye-catching than a traditional chalkboard presentation. To get the class's attention just turn on the projector!

- Make your own permanent transparencies from printed materials by using your school's heat-process copying machine. Make full-color transparencies by placing clear Contact paper (purchased from any variety store) on any clay-based paper. Wash away the paper and the colored image remains on the Contact.

  - To determine whether or not paper is clay-based, put a piece of transparent tape ("Scotch Tape") on a piece of printed matter. Dip it in water and soak. If the paper is clay-coated, the picture or printing will adhere to the tape when the paper washes away.

  - If you want to learn more about making and labelling transparencies, ask your local 3M representative to give a workshop at your school.

  - To mount your homemade transparencies, make frames from old file folders. Staple or tape the transparency inside. Label the tab. Seal the flap of an envelope onto the frame if you have descriptive material that should be filed with it. Flip the envelope to one side when showing the transparency.

  - Cut different sizes of the same object from construction paper. Use these figures on the overhead projector to illustrate comparison: big, bigger, biggest. Tall, taller, tallest.

  - Cut out the symbol p. Let children manipulate it on the overhead to make p, b, and d. This is good drill for the child who has difficulty distinguishing between similar letters.

  - Wet a leaf. Rub it with a wire brush. Project the leaf on the overhead to illustrate veining.

  - The overhead projector is wonderful for math. Put 15 paperclips on it and ask a child to illustrate a number fact by moving the paperclips into two groups. Children at their seats can record the fact on paper. See how many different facts the children can make using the same 15 paperclips.

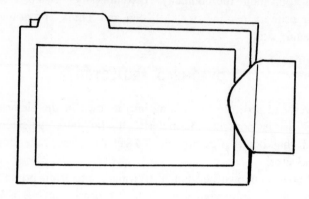

- Put coins on the projector. Have children recognize them by their relative size. Then call on a child to give the total value of the coins.
■ Order Spirit/Tran Masters from

> Instructo Products Co.
>
> Philadelphia
>
> Pennsylvania

- Write on the Spirit/Tran as you would on a regular ditto. Run it through the duplicating machine to make seatwork for the class. Then put the master copy on the overhead projector. It becomes a transparency. The class can check its answers as you work the problem in grease pencil on the master copy.
- Make a grid pattern on the Spirit/Tran. Play a "following directions" game with the class. Let each child move a paper clip on his copy of the grid, according to directions: "one space down, two spaces to the right." Turn on the overhead and show where the clip should be.
- Use the same procedure to develop map skills. Draw a map of the neighborhood. Distribute dittoed copies to the class. A paper clip or a cut out figure can represent each child. Give directions: "Start at the school, walk two blocks north, turn right, walk three blocks. Where are you?" Turn on the projector and let them check their position with yours.
■ If you use Scott-Foresman readers, you'll save time and accomplish more if you have a set of Flipatrans. All the materials from the teacher's guide (which you'd ordinarily write

on the board), is copied on transparencies and filed in a handy binder.

- If you use another reading program, copy material from the guide onto acetate sheets with audio-visual pencils. Replace one sheet with another, on the overhead, instead of erasing the board and tediously copying down another column of words. You can save the acetate sheets to use again if you plan to repeat the work with another group.

■ For more ideas on how to use both opaque and overhead projectors, send 25¢ for "101 Teaching Ideas" to:

> Charles Beseler Company
> Projection Division
> 206 (D) S. 18th St.
> East Orange, New Jersey

EARPHONES

To make effective use of tape recorder, Language Master, and phonograph (and t.v., if you have a jack installed) you must have ear phones.

- Invest in padded ones. Children can listen in comfort for longer periods of time.

Earphones should be available for use with the tape recorder, Language Master, phonograph and TV.

- Look for the new wireless seats. The room is permanently wired (for a few cents) and the wire, rather than the earphones, is plugged into the machine. Anyone within the circumference of the wire can listen if he wears earphones. Children are free to move around and work in widely separated parts of the room.

CARRELS

Look for room dividers, study carrels, or table dividers if you want to free your children from distractions. Write for information about Porto-Booths from:

Vision Manufacturing Co.
P.O. Box 360
Bartlett, Illinois

One set of porto-booths can be set up in a matter of seconds to form two to eight individual study carrels. They can be made to fit either round or rectangular table tops. Or try making your own dividers by cutting sections from cardboard cartons to fit your table.

Obtaining the Equipment

What if your school doesn't have the equipment you want? BEG or BORROW!

Borrow from other schools. Does the local high school have a film loop projector? Make arrangements to use it. Does a neighboring school have the Controlled Reader? Ask if you can borrow it for a month. Is the Speech or French teacher using the Language Master? Would she be willing to let you use it a few hours a week? If there isn't one in the district, talk the

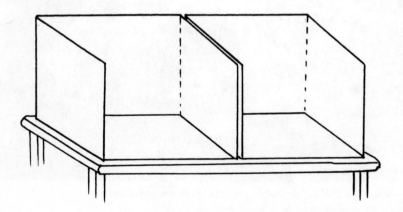

language and speech departments into sharing the cost of purchase with your school!

Do you have an Audio-Visual Coordinator for your district? It may be more efficient and cheaper in the long run to have someone to take charge of all audio-visual equipment. Some materials should be in each classroom or building, but some can easily be shared. Investigate the possibility of using Federal Funds for the records, films and tapes you want.

Interest the P.T.A. in purchasing audio-visual equipment as a gift to the school. Organize a Materials Fair for a P.T.A. meeting. Invite the superintendent and school board members. Ask company representatives to demonstrate the newest machines. Impress everyone with the variety of new teaching tools available. Sell them on how much more effective you can be, given the right equipment!

How does the right audio-visual equipment make you a more effective teacher?

It helps you individualize your school program. You can provide work for children who are ready for new concepts and enrichment. You can provide meaningful drill for children who need it. While you teach a reading group, a committee watches a science filmstrip; a child practices his vocabulary cards on the Language Master; other children are drilled on math facts by record; a student who's been absent is given a spelling test by tape recorder. The class is busy, quiet, and everyone is learning at his own particular level.

You are following sound educational principles, too, when you use equipment that is self-correcting. A child learns more surely when his mistakes are caught immediately. Language Master cards, records, and tape allow children to check their own work. Might not these be better teaching tools than seat-work assignments that aren't handed back or corrected until the next day?

Mechanical equipment fascinates children. It offers a new and novel approach to learning. With it you may find just the right way to reach the child who hasn't been taught by conventional methods. It's well worth a try!

Of particular help to the classroom teacher is Herbert Scuorzo's PRACTICAL AUDIO-VISUAL HANDBOOK FOR TEACHERS (West Nyack: Parker Publishing Co., Inc., 1967.)

20

The Senses: Tools for Learning

Karen Hillerud Rush

> *Nothing is in the intellect which*
> *was not first in the senses . . .*
> *Aristotle*

ABOUT THE AUTHOR

Karen Hillerud Rush received her Bachelor of Arts degree from Carleton College in Northfield, Minnesota and the Master of Education from Cornell University. She has continued her graduate work at the University of Rochester and Brockport Teachers College. She was a member of the Board of Trustees for the Rochester Montessori School in Rochester, New York. She has taught elementary, junior and senior high school subjects in the states of New York, New Jersey and Virginia, and for the Dependents Schools in Germany. Mrs. Rush contributed material in music and language arts to *The Come-Alive Classroom*.

Each of the five senses has a special function for perception. Therefore each must be trained and refined in order to furnish a solid basis for the development of intelligence.

Prior to entering school, children express their interest in the world in numerous spontaneous ways. Inside the classroom, the teacher must direct this energy and curiosity into educational channels while encouraging and enriching the independence of the learner.

When equipped with strong sensory skills, children are able to perceive more clearly and express themselves with a vocabulary developed from describing, classifying and comparing stimuli perceived by the senses. It is through these means that they are better prepared to interpret the written exercises and abstract concepts encountered in textbooks. Also, they are more aware of their environment, learning much from their daily "practical life" experiences.

Fortunately, it is not difficult to interest a child in work that stimulates his senses. Children of all ages are fascinated by games and exercises designed to sharpen the senses.

Math, music, art, language arts, science, and social studies—the entire curriculum is associated with sensory strength. Thus, activities in sight, sound, taste, touch, and smell which *relate to the curriculum* have been compiled in this chapter. Hopefully, they will stimulate more ideas and variations to aid children in the development and refinement of their senses.

EXERCISES WITH SIGHT

Measurement

The following exercises were developed to refine the child's ability to recognize and judge distance and sizes. They also illustrate how terrain and shape can affect estimates. The exercises have been successful with upper grade children, but could be adapted for any child who understands units of measurement. Children have chosen these exercises for recess activities.

ESTIMATING DISTANCE

Exercises

Materials: Six to nine colorful stakes at least 3' long

Yardsticks and tape measure

Chalk

A field, playground or parking lot with few or no trees or other markings

The teacher draws a line or places a marker at the standing line. Then he sets the stakes at 1—10—20 yard intervals. Children form groups of four: one child at each end of a tape measure, one reading the measurement and one recording it. Groups begin at the standing line and measure the distance to each stake. When finished, they compare their measurements with the actual measurements and make necessary corrections. Children may then stand at the line, look at the stakes, and "memorize" the distances.

Repeat this exercise several times, changing the space intervals of the stakes.

The teacher places the standing line and sets the stakes at various intervals. Children form groups and estimate measurements. Then they measure the actual distance to each stake and compare their estimates to the correct measurements.

After experience with these exercises, the children can place the standing line and set the stakes.

Find a site where there are trees, shrubs, rugged terrain or other diversions. Place standing line and stakes. Children form groups, estimate distances, then measure and compare. Discuss the effect site has on perception.

ESTIMATING DISTANCE IN AN ENCLOSED AREA

Exercises
Materials: Chalk or marker
Yardstick and tape measure

Draw a box 10′ x 10′ in the gymnasium or on the playground. Have children measure the box and walk around the lines. Let them pace off to see how close they can come to the actual measurement of the 10′ x 10′ box.

Ask children to estimate the size of the classroom. Let them pace the distance, then measure and compare the three figures. Encourage children to experiment with this exercise at home.

MEASUREMENT OF OBJECTS

Exercises
Materials: Ruler, yardstick and tape measure
Unmarked sticks cut to measured sizes
(inch, foot, yard)
Construction paper of 1″ width and
cut to various measured lengths
(1″, 3″, 9″, etc.)

First, teach children the sizes of the measured rods or sticks. Then let them compare objects in the room (pictures, desks, chairs) to the sticks. Ask them to make an accurate measurement and to compare the figures.

After experience with this exercise have children mentally estimate sizes and check estimates by measuring.

Number each piece of construction paper and record the number and its size on a master chart. Children estimate the size of the pieces, then measure and compare their findings with the master chart. (This can be a game prepared by the children.)

DISCRIMINATION OF SIZE

Exercises

Materials: Different shaped gallon, quart, pint, cup containers

Standard measuring cups graded to gallon

Children measure the amount of liquid each standard measuring container holds. (Food coloring adds interest.) Afterwards, they estimate the approximate sizes of the different shaped containers. They check themselves by filling the containers from the standard measuring cups.

Materials: Boxes or blocks of the same size

Boxes or blocks of various sizes

Place the same sized boxes at different distances. Ask children to guess which are larger and which smaller. Collect the boxes and compare. Use same procedure with boxes of various sizes.

Eye puzzle books are good sources for experiences with perception and actual sizes.

Perception of Color

The following exercises were developed to refine the child's ability to recognize and remember colors, to increase his awareness of color and to develop an appreciation for its uses. Children at every level have been interested in these exercises.

Exercises

Materials: Spools of thread with labels removed. Prepare two sets (A and B) with 8 shades of color. Sets can be built up to 64 colors, 8 shades of 8 colors. (Children must hold spools on wooden areas to protect colors.)

Paints and brushes

Arrange Set A in chromatic scale from lightest to darkest shades. Children practice independently with Set B, arranging the colors from lightest to darkest and comparing results with Set A.

Children match the colors in Set A with those of Set B. Game variations might include placing Set B in another part of the room and asking the child to "memorize" a color in Set A and find its match in Set B. A child might select a color and carry it with him, searching for matching colors indoors and out. When he finds one, he can check against the color spool in his pocket.

The teacher or children mix tempera colors and create a color chart. Children experiment with color by mixing the paints until their colors match those on the chart.

Because of the repetitive nature of these exercises many children develop an accurate memory for color.

Accuracy of Memory

This activity is popular at all grade levels. It gives children experience in observation and memorization.

Exercise
Materials: A tray with familiar items (soap, comb, napkin, dish, book, models, etc.)

The filled tray is shown to the children for 30 seconds. It is removed. After waiting one minute, the children list everything they remember seeing on the tray. The tray is returned and the lists checked.

Appreciation of Cultural Values

These activities are designed to help children become aware of the fact that values are culturally determined . . . what is "pretty" to one group may be "ugly" to another. These will also allow the child to recognize that his own visual values will change as his society's cultural values change or as his experiences broaden.

Exercises
Place different works of art around the room—primitive, Oriental, renaissance, modern, graphic, children's art, pop art, representative art, etc. Ask children to discuss their feelings about each work. Discuss the cultures that appreciate the art.

Prepare an exhibit of styles of western world clothing from past to present. Point up changes within the last 10 years. Help children see that a culture can change its values of style and fashion within centuries and over short periods of time.

Use other ideas for discussion such as clothing styles from around the world, architectural styles, etc.

EXERCISES WITH HEARING

Discrimination of Sound

The following activities are intended to refine the child's ability to perceive and appreciate different types of sounds. They are applicable at all grade levels.

Exercises

Materials: Two identical sets of six closed containers* filled with different substances (gravel, sand, salt, beads, oatmeal, etc.)

*Covered containers of any type will do . . . film cans, salt shakers, pill boxes . . .

Children take a container from Set A, shake it, and match its sounds to a container in Set B. They may then open the containers to check their findings.

Children place the Set A containers in order from softest to loudest sounds. They can check themselves by comparing their arrangements with Set B which is in order.

Materials: Various band instruments

Phonograph records: *Peter and the Wolf* by Prokofiev (primary grades) *Young People's Guide to the Orchestra* by Benjamin Britten (Upper grades)

Introduce children to instruments of the band by playing the notes while they watch. (Perhaps a band instructor would assist with this presentation.) Ask children to identify the sounds with their eyes closed. Then play the phonograph record and ask them to identify the instruments they hear.

Using a piano or pitch pipe, play the regular scale and then the chromatic scale. Discuss the notes. Then play two notes (same or different). Ask children to determine whether notes are higher or lower.

Materials: Recordings of:
Greensleeves (with guitar accom-
paniment)
Fantasia on Greensleeves by Ralph
Vaughn Williams
Rite of Spring by Igor Stravinsky

Play a piece of music with an easy melody—*Greensleeves*. Then play
Fantasia on Greensleeves. Discuss the similarities and differences of sound
and mood.

Play excerpts from *Rite of Spring*. Compare it to *Fantasia on Greensleeves*. Discuss the different sounds, moods and interpretations in the
music. Note that these sounds all come from the same notes played in different relationships.

Cultural Values

These activities are highly successful with upper grade classes and can
easily be adapted for primary grades. They help children recognize the
ways that appreciation for sound varies with different cultures.

Exercises

Materials: Recordings of music from other countries—Orient, Greece, India, South
and North America, Africa and
Europe—folk, popular, classical.
Recordings of people speaking various
languages.
U.S. Committee for UNICEF has a
series entitled *Hi Neighbor* with
songs and dances from other
countries. Order from:
UNICEF
United Nations
New York, New York 10017

Play excerpts from the music of different countries. Identify the geographical areas on a map or globe. From what the children have learned
in social studies, can they see any relationship between the music and the
culture of a people? the music and the climate?

Play language records. Note that the voice changes with the change in
language. Note that certain sounds which are pleasant to people of one
language might be unpleasant to people of another.

Play city and country sounds. Discuss effect of different noises on someone from either environment.

Ability to Listen

The ability to listen to, organize and remember sounds is vital in the
classroom. The following activities are designed to help children pay attention creatively.

Exercises
Materials: Tape recorder and sound effects record.

Tape record sounds that denote a specific action or activity. Play the tape
and ask children to write a short paragraph or story mentioning the sounds
they heard. Replay the tape and let
them check to see how many sounds
they included in their story.

Read an article to the class from the
weekly newspaper. Ask children to
rewrite what they remember. Read the
article again and let children check
their memories.

EXERCISES WITH SMELL

Discrimination of Odors

These activities apply to all grade levels and aid the child in the refinement of his ability to distinguish odors.

Exercise
Materials: Small bottles (salt shakers, baby food
jars, pill bottles)
Spices, oils, herbs, catsup, mustard,
vinegar, perfumes, flowers, etc.
Cotton

Pour liquids into the cotton placed in the bottles. Solids are placed under
a thin layer of cotton so they cannot be identified by sight. Label the odor
on the bottom of the container Children identify the odors and check themselves.

Appreciation of Cultural Values

It is important that children recognize that appreciation for certain odors is related to environment and experience. All grade levels can be given this awareness.

> *Exercises*
> Discuss natural odors in relation to environment:
> a. Farm odors—orchard, grove, hay, manure, etc.
> b. City odors—exhaust, smoke, paper mills, etc.
> c. Cooking odors—grease, pie, bread, cabbage, cheese

Discuss culturally appreciated odors, such as perfumes, incense, and spiced foods. Discuss the idea of masking odors, such as body odors, cooking odors, exhaust fumes.

Discuss the value of odors, for instance, to determine the freshness of foods, to determine cleanliness, and to whet appetites.

Children can be helped to recognize that physical and mental circumstances affect the perception and interpretation of odors. Discuss illness and odors; stomach aches, head colds, fever. Discuss a person's state of mind and his reaction to odors: hunger and smell of food, flowers at a wedding, flowers at a funeral, etc.

EXERCISES WITH TOUCH

These activities refine children's ability to use touch as a means of determining the qualities of an object, and to introduce them to the tremendous adjustments that must be made by those who have lost the sense of sight.

Introduce the unit by reading about a blind person who developed his sense of touch. A favorite with children is *Follow My Leader* by James B. Garfield (New York: The Viking Press, 1957). Any grade level book on Helen Keller would be suitable also.

> *Materials:* Blindfold (masks or hats pulled over the eyes, or the child closing his eyes would be sufficient)
> Drawstring bag
> Collection of fabrics cut in small squares
> Small familiar shapes (doll furniture,

eraser, model car)
Braille alphabet cards—Obtained from:
American Printing House for the
Blind
1839 Frankfort Avenue
Louisville, Kentucky 40206

Masks or hats can be substituted for conventional blindfolds.

Children are blindfolded and asked to identify the objects in the draw-string bag.

Children are introduced to the Braille alphabet card. After learning some of the basic letters, they might try to read Braille while blindfolded. They can try to make their own Braille readers by poking pins through cardboard.

Children place paper over different surfaces and rub crayon or pencil over them to see the different texture marks. They can then run their hands over the surface to see if the texture can be felt.

Children learn the names and textures of different fabrics by sight and touch: corduroy, velvet, cotton, wool, satin, silk, linen, burlap, etc. They are then blindfolded and asked to identify the fabrics by touch and to indicate the quality of the material: fine, coarse, soft, smooth, etc.

Materials: Blindfold
Wooden or plastic geometric shapes:
star, rectangle, square, triangle, etc.

Teach the children the names of the shapes. Let them touch and feel their outlines. Blindfold a child and let him identify the shape by touch. He can remove the blindfold to check his identification.

> Materials: Variety of seeds, paper cups or muffin
> tin
> Blindfold

Introduce children to a variety of seeds. Let them identify each by sight and touch. After blindfolding, let the children sort the seeds in paper cups or a muffin tin.

> Materials: A blindfold and small objects of wood,
> glass, plastic, tin, etc.

Let children discuss and describe the different objects while looking at them. When blindfolded, let them handle the objects again. Discuss the properties that cannot be "seen" such as thermal properties and texture.

> Materials: Modeling clay and blindfold

Blindfold the child and let him make clay figures using only the sense of touch.

Discrimination of Weight

It is important for children to realize that some qualities cannot always be seen but must be sensed by touch. These activities refine the child's ability to estimate weights and to give him experience working with weighing devices.

> Exercises
> Materials: Different woods, the same size and
> color but having different weights . .
> (chestnut, oak, poplar, maple,
> balsa)
> Scale for weighing the wood pieces

Ask children to handle the wood and determine a weight difference. Blindfold a child and let him determine which is heavier by raising and lowering the two pieces of wood in his hands. After removing the blindfold, he can verify his decision by weighing the wood on the scale.

> Materials: Objects weighing the same but differ-

ing in size (salt and oatmeal, small
bit of lead and sack of sugar, etc.)

Let children hold materials and determine which weigh the same. They can check by using the scale. Show children how distribution of weight affects estimations.

> *Materials:* Frozen juice cans filled to different
> heights with sand, and covered with
> identical covers.

Let children hold the different cans to determine weight and arrange them from lightest to heaviest can. They can check by weighing the cans.

EXERCISES WITH TASTE

These exercises give children experience in identification of flavors and can teach them the names of the qualities of flavors.

> *Exercises*
> Materials: Sugar (sweet), Salt (saline), Lemon
> (sour), Cooking oil (bland)

Place a drop of liquid on each child's tongue, identifying it as sweet, saline, sour, or bland. Ask the children to name other liquids which have these qualities. Fill medicine dropper bottles with the four flavors and let children experiment by themselves. Label the bottles so they can check their findings.

For an exercise in cultural values, the children can discuss eating unusual foods: shortbreads, tongue, raw eggs, liver, ants, different milks. Sample oriental cooking, Indian recipes with curry, Mexican dishes with hot peppers, etc.

Since the senses are avenues through which the child gains most of his knowledge, an important duty of the teacher is to stimulate interest in regular and systematic development of these powers.

When the children become independently interested in developing their powers, the teacher has succeeded!

21

Learning Reinforcement: Games in the Classroom

Dale S. Devine

ABOUT THE AUTHOR

Dale Devine received her Bachelor of Arts in English degree from Carleton College and the Master of Education degree from Cornell University. She has taught second and third graders in the Irondequoit Schools of Rochester, New York, in Kaiserslautern, Germany with the U.S. Army Dependents Schools and in the Hinsdale, Illinois school system. She contributed material to the book *The Come-Alive Classroom* and co-authored *"From Crib to Kindergarten, a Primer for Parents"* which won first prize in *Scholastic Teacher's* 1968 Promising New Practices in Elementary Education Contest. Mrs. Devine has given PTA programs and conducted teacher-workshops for Hinsdale elementary teachers. She was chosen as the Outstanding Young Educator of the Year of 1969 for the Hinsdale-Clarendon Hills Area.

Games in the classroom are wonderful "cover-up" for otherwise routine drill. They are perfect fillers for spare moments, they help maintain classroom discipline, develop leadership, stimulate creativity:

- When the music teacher is late arriving—*play a game.*
- A child has problems and needs immediate assistance —*let the class play a game.*
- Some children finish a project early—*send them to the board to play a game.*

The so-called "extra" minutes in a day can add up to a lot of learning reinforcement if they're used for games. They're a great way to create enthusiasm!

There are many good learning games on the market (Quizmo, Lotto, Equations) but often those with the most lasting appeal—those which best meet the needs and interests of the class—are teacher-made. And games which require no materials (or nothing more than paper and pencil or chalk and board) can be played on the spur of the moment: even a minute or two can be put to use if you don't need to pass out materials.

Eventually a class can run itself on games. Individuals and groups will go off by themselves to play games—and all the while they are learning.

■ Once you have played a game a few times, let the children take turns leading it. Make a mental note of which child to call on when your attention must be elsewhere.

> • Make written notes in lesson plans for substitutes. If a substitute finishes her lesson sooner than you'd planned, have her call on a child to lead a game—then let her sit back and learn!

■ A good game, like a good recipe, can be dressed up to fit any occasion. Once you find a format that appeals to your group, play it for all its worth. Change it to fit the subject, the season, or the class's mood. In one class, THE game (not charades, but a teacher-made math game) is requested for recess and even for entertainment at class parties!

■ If you're creative with your games, your children soon will be. You'll find them suggesting changes which will make the game more exciting or more appropriate to their current interests.

■ Establish specific rules for each game. Establish ground rules for all games:

> 1. Anyone who does not follow the rules is immediately disqualified.
> 2. A point is taken from any team that is unduly noisy.
> 3. A point is taken from any team that displays poor sportsmanship to another team or to any of its OWN members.

Establish ground rules for yourself which apply to all games:

> 1. Let every child think he has a chance to win—no game is fun unless one has a reasonable expectation of winning.
> 2. Intersperse easier questions with more difficult ones and call on slower children for these.
> 3. Have slower pupils start the game, when the work is easiest (as in counting games or alphabetizing).

4. Pair children of similar abilities; match teams as to the number of faster children on each.

5. Give all children an opportunity to show that they know the answer. If contestants are writing on the board, let the children at their seats indicate the answer on paper or by holding up the correct number of fingers. Let them whisper in your ear as you walk by. Tell them you can see who knows the answer by looking in their eyes!

6. Have as many teams as possible. Four teams are better than two if it means more turns for each child.

7. Let a loser save face. When a child misses, let him choose the next contestant. The child and the class focus attention on his choice, not his error.

8. Give children an opportunity to re-enter the game once they've been out: after a suitable period of good behavior if they've been disqualified; by giving the correct answer when someone misses. A child who has no hope of being back in the game loses interest and therefore is no longer learning from the game.

9. Give the problem first, THEN call on someone.

10. Make a practice of calling on children who are attentive and well-mannered.

■ DIRECTIONS is a good game for any age group. Give a list of three directions (Touch your head, clap three times, run to the door). Then call on a child to do all three. Don't repeat. If the first child misses, call on another. The more children called on, the harder it is to remember the original directions (it's a good idea to jot them down so YOU remember). This is excellent for practice in listening to and following instructions.

■ MENTAL GYMNASTICS exercises "the mind." Call out a problem: "5 times 2, take away 3, add 4, multiply by 7." Call on a child to supply the answer. Make "times zero" the last instruction a few times and everyone will soon catch on to the "trick" of multiplying by zero.

■ THE MATH GAME, which can be suited to any grade, is played on the board. Two contestants stand with their backs to the board as the teacher fills in the boxes. At the signal, the children turn around and begin to work, starting at the outside and working toward the center. The first one to fill in his blank square with the correct numeral is the winner. As soon as the contestants turn their backs on the "audience," children at their desks can raise the correct number of fingers to indicate they've solved the equation. While it is possible to indicate the symbol, it challenges the children more, and increases their mathematical vocabulary, if you put the numerals on the board and make them figure out the process by saying "Find the missing addend (or product, remainder, sum)."

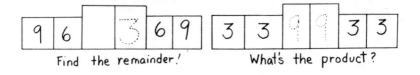

Find the remainder!   What's the product?

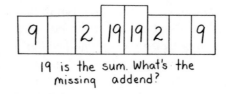

19 is the sum. What's the
missing addend?

This game can be made more festive:

Fill in the sum

What's the
product?

What's
the
remainder?

■ RELAY RACE: Another simple drill game is to divide the class into three or four teams and send them to the board. At a given signal, the first member of each team writes a numeral on the board (whatever they need practice on—1, 2, 3, 4; 1000, 10001, 10002, I, II, III, IV)—then runs to the end of his line. Once a numeral is written teammates can give oral help and it can be changed (take advantage of team spirit to let pupils teach one another). When the teacher calls stop, each team counts to see how many numerals they have written without an error.

■ PLACE VALUE CONTEST: Make number sets of the numerals from 0–9. Divide the class into teams (ideally of 10 each). Make sure each child has at least one card. If you have extra, give to the children who need the most drill on place value. Make a station at the board near each team. Indicate positions for thousands, hundreds, tens and ones. Call a number. The first team to be in correct position scores a point. Again, let team members help one another. Be sure, of course, to have a numeral in only one place each time (1345, not 1335).

■ SWIM THE ATLANTIC: The only prop you need for one good game is a rug or even an imaginary spot on the floor. The area between sides is the Atlantic Ocean which must be swum, or a downhill slope which must be skiied without falling or an icy pond which must be traversed without skating onto thin ice. As soon as a child gives a correct response, he moves to the other side. It's a good game to play when you wish to make a quick check to see who is catching on to a new concept.

This game is equally at home on a chalk board or in a reading group. A child goes from a sinking ship to a tropical isle by way of a raft of words—or he moves into the pilot seat of a jetliner by adding suffixes to words written on the jet's stream. If there is time for a second turn, the child on the island can "earn" a fire, palm tree, coconuts, etc.

Over The Raft to Safety!

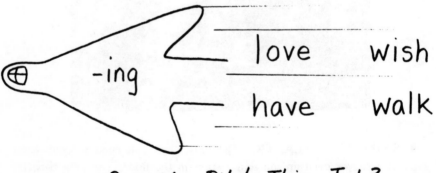

Can You Pilot This Jet?

■ VARIATIONS ON TWENTY QUESTIONS: Improve the children's questioning techniques with a variation of 20 Questions. Place any common object in a cardboard box. Allow Team A to see the object and let Team B ask questions which can be answered only by "yes" or "no." The teacher can be the moderator and the whole class can ask questions to speed things up. You may want to introduce some discussion of the appropriateness of the questions after each game. Write on the board any properties of the object as they are determined by the questions.

■ VARIATIONS ON BUZZ: Many other parlor games can be converted to classroom use. The old game of Buzz can be played in a circle. "1, 2, 3, 4, Buzz" or "1001, 1002, 1003, 1004, Buzz." Children who miss go into the center. The child in the center who first calls out the correct answer when a child makes a mistake, can replace him in the circle. This same game can be played without the "buzz" to practice skip counting: 2, 4, 6, 8, 10, 12 . . . or 5, 10, 15, 20. It can be played to see how far the class can count without making a mistake.

■ MY GRANDMOTHER WENT TO EUROPE (OR MY TEACHER WENT TO SCHOOL) and with her she took an apple, a banana, a cat . . . This game is good practice for alphabetizing. Have slower children near the start so they'll have less to remember. The first child says something which begins with a, the next child repeats the word and adds one which starts with b and so on. It helps to have an alphabet chart in sight.

■ I'M THINKING OF SOMETHING. Another word game is I'm Thinking of Something in the room that rhymes with bear:

> Is it chair?
> That rhymes but it's not what I'm thinking of.
> Is it hair?
> That's it. Now it's your turn.

(The child whispers his pair of rhyming words in the teacher's ear. This assures a good rhyme and thwarts any attempt to change words once the questioning has begun.)

This can also be I'm thinking of something that starts (or ends) like "cat" or "I'm thinking of something in the room that is rectangular in shape."

■ HANGMAN, without the hanging or the man, is an excellent spelling game. Write a word or sentence on the board, but put blanks for each letter. With sentences, indicate the end of words with slash marks. Use spelling words or words from social studies or science units. Discuss the logic of the game. Help children discover that vowels are always a good first choice; that some consonants appear more frequently than others. A child calls off letters until he calls one *not* in the sentence. That letter is recorded on the board and another child continues. Children soon begin to visualize the total look of a word. Non-spellers learn that TH__ calls for an E and the A__D usually means and. This is a fun way of giving directions: For instance, the blanks: __ __ __ __/__ __ __/__ __ __ __/__ __ __ __/ __ __ __ __ __ become TAKE/OUT/YOUR/MATH/BOOKS and is a novel introduction to the next subject.

■ SHAPES: Another spelling game in language arts, social studies or science is to draw the shapes of the words on the board and let children fill them in.

Emphasis can be placed on vowels and consonants:

■ DICTIONARY RACES: Dictionary skills can be reinforced by dictionary races. Divide the class into teams, or let each child have a dictionary. Call out a word (be sure you've checked to make sure it appears in their dictionaries). The first to find it wins. Or the first team to find it scores a point. Children soon learn it is faster to estimate where M is in the dictionary than to start at A and work back.

■ ADD-QUICK: Bring one of the grocery store add-quick gadgets to class. The teacher or a student writes a four-place number on the board and on the adder. The person holding the adder says, "I'm going to add four tens" (and clicks the button for the tens place four times) "and two ones" (and clicks the ones place button). Children mentally figure the new number, then see if their answer matches the adder. This can also be played in twos.

If you use your imagination, anything that requires an answer from a child can be a game. In reading group, let them keep track of the number of correct responses they make by writing down a letter of their name each time they answer correctly. At the end of the reading time, see if anyone has spelled his whole name. Or draw circles on the board for each child. Add a feature each time a person responds correctly. Once you catch on to the game of making up—or adapting—games, routine classwork will become much more fun!

Accentuating the Positive: A Word from the Principal

Elizabeth Hobbs

> *Morale is a delicate plant that grows*
> *slowly in an atmosphere of mutual respect.*
> *Kimball Wiles*

ABOUT THE AUTHOR

Elizabeth Hobbs was graduated from the University of Florida with BA and MED degrees. She taught in both elementary and junior high schools in Jacksonville, Florida, and in the Bartow Senior High School in Bartow, Florida. After twenty years in a teaching career, she entered the administrative field, acting as the principal of the Ortega and John N.C. Stockton elementary schools. She has contributed poetry and literary articles to *The Educational Forum, The Clearing House, Scimitar and Song, Poetry Public* and the *National Poetry Anthology*.

In schools where the teaching personnel have the required educational qualifications, broad cultural backgrounds, a genuine concern for children, and zeal for their chosen work, good schools just naturally ensue.

All teachers have goals and sets of values by which they are guided. The conditions which create harmonious working relationships within the faculty are the same which confront the teacher in his classroom. The principal with his faculty—the teacher with his class—meet similar challenges in the day-to-day life of the school. By "accentuating the positive," "minimizing the negative," the principal, teachers and children are stimulated to work toward their fullest potential.

Do You Accentuate the Positive?

The superior teacher expresses confidence in the children's ability to perform their work. He *tells* them, verbally and by his *actions*, that he *knows* they will do their best, and he works to develop within them the kind of moral and spiritual values acceptable to the society in which they are living.

- He expresses his appreciation to the children for striving toward the highest goals which they are able to reach.
- He assures them that he will do his utmost to assist them in the accomplishment of their best work.

If children feel they can depend upon the teacher, that he really appreciates their dignity and worth as individuals, then they can work and cooperate in a comfortable tension-free atmosphere.

Is Praise Important?

All persons work better with praise than without it. The teacher should utilize every opportunity to give deserved and well-earned praise. Children truly appreciate being told that what they have done is good. It is not possible to give too much sincere praise.

Are Your Criticisms Made in Private?

All people—adults and children—appreciate constructive criticism made in private. Destructive criticism which destroys the child's morale and offers no suggestions for reaching solutions can be devastating. No child appreciates being rebuked before other children. The tactful teacher can make criticisms in such a way that there are no hurt feelings when the talk is concluded and both agree to work out problems together.

Are You a Good Listener?

To be of positive assistance to children, the teacher should be a good listener. He needs to remember that children, as well as adults, have many problems. Nothing is so helpful as feeling free to discuss a problem with a trusted person.

The Open Door Policy should include parents as well. By listening to both sides of a situation and by contributing to sympathetic discussions, the teacher can aid in diminishing the anxiety of the parents and the children, and help pull problems back into proper perspective.

How Is Your Democracy?

The superior teacher lets children know that their ideas, suggestions and feelings have a part in the decisions which affect their lives and working conditions in the classroom.

- He gives them the opportunity for decision-making by the formulation of committees: classroom student-government committees, social committees, library committees, research committees, and others.
- He encourages round-table discussions, voting on policies, participation in the routine responsibilities of the classroom.

How Can Your Students Achieve Recognition?

To enable children to achieve the recognition which they deserve, the teacher, working with the principal, should seek favorable publicity for the school.

- Announcements may be made at PTA and Dads' Club meetings about outstanding creative units occurring in the classrooms.
- Parents may be invited to view the work in classrooms, in the cafeteria, in corridors or in the library.
- Parents may be invited to assembly programs.
- Upon the culmination of an unusual unit of work, newspaper reporters may be invited to participate in a final activity: a foreign dinner prepared by children and room mothers, or an unusual field trip. Sometimes the reporters can be persuaded to join in the Canadian or western folk dancing, or the types of games played by the pioneers. Reporters who observe and participate write excellent articles for the local papers!
- Parents working in PTA and Dads' Club can assist in securing publicity for many school projects. For example, Garden Circle members in the community may help sponsor a Junior Garden Club within a school or a single classroom. The activities of the Junior Garden Club can be reported along with those of the adult group.

Are Your Children Allowed to Be Creative?

A flexible teacher who wants to see subject matter given sparkle should encourage and be willing for children to embark upon original projects.

Sometimes the entire school can become involved in an overall project started by one grade. One such project was initiated by a fifth grade class while they were studying Hawaii. They invited the other two fifth grades to join in and work out an original drama for assembly. Sixth graders asked if they could participate. Soon the third and fourth asked if they could make costumes to wear on assembly day. First and second graders made paper hibiscus blossoms to wear to the program and drew murals for the cafeteria bulletin boards. The librarian displayed books, pamphlets, travel folders, records and filmstrips about Hawaii. The custodial staff helped with greenery for the stage and cafeteria lunch tables. Lunch on assembly day was typically Hawaiian, complete with Hawaiian punch and poi. The menu had been worked out by a fifth grade committee several weeks prior to the program. Parents, county supervisors and reporters were invited to Hawaiian Day.

Original projects, committee projects, all-class or all-school projects can carry children far beyond the walls of the classroom in their learning experiences.

Conclusions

The elementary school teacher can create harmonious working conditions in the classroom by consistently remembering to accentuate the good points of each child and to minimize the weak ones. With the use of constant, *sincere* praise and recognition when deserved, the positive factors will be practiced so frequently that the negative factors will recede and eventually be overcome—or at least reduced to their proper proportions!

Index